Frontispiece: The Good Life, West Coast Style. Children's librarian for San Mateo County, California, Nancy Schimmel has just taught an origami class at the El Granada branch; now, across the street at the Pacific Ocean, she helps two beautiful young Californians test their paper birds.

LIBRARY LIFE —
AMERICAN STYLE

A Journalist's Field Report

by

ARTHUR PLOTNIK

The Scarecrow Press, Inc.

Metuchen, N.J.   1975

Chapters One through Seven are based on articles
which appeared originally in Wilson Library Bulletin, © 1971, 1972, 1973 and 1974 by The H. W.
Wilson Company, and are reprinted by permis-
sion of the Company.

Library of Congress Cataloging in Publication Data

Plotnik, Arthur.
    Library life--American style.

    "Chapters one through seven are based on articles
which appeared originally in Wilson Library
Bulletin."
    Includes bibliographical references and index.
    1. Libraries--United States. I. Title.
Z731.P663   021'.00973   75-16280
ISBN 0-8108-0852-8

CONTENTS

ACKNOWLEDGMENTS

I owe thanks to many more than I can mention. Among those who receive no recognition in the text of this book are the following, to whom I am especially grateful:

Wm. R. Eshelman   Agnes Griffen
Leo M. Weins   Gil McNamee
John Jamieson   Peggy O'Donnell
Carla Alexander   Nan Vaaler
Norm and Dallas Shaffer   Simon Taub
Kay Haas   Meta Von Borstel Plotnik
William and Lucy Alexander
The Nebraska and West Virginia State Library Commissions

SWEET LAND OF LIBRARIES, OF THEE I SING!

My search for the Great American Library Dream probably began on my analyst's couch ten years ago in 1964. The search is far from over; I hope it will not lead me back there. It was then that I was seeking a career which, unlike newspaper reporting and hack writing, had something solid and enduring to it, positive and humanistic goals in which one could believe. "Librarianship is that career!" said an editorial in Esquire at the time (it was during National Library Week), and even my shrink had to agree it wasn't a bad idea for getting me out of my directionless doldrums and general, mid-twenties, post-Kennedy malaise.

So I applied to library school and began to dream about the happy perpetuation of civilization via the circulation desk, of libraries beloved by their communities, of librarians (myself?) whose only failing would be to have but two arms and one mind with which to serve the ceaseless intellectual demands of a grateful public. In fellowship applications I wrote of books and people and ardent intermediaries between them. I visited small public libraries and saw what I wanted to see: good souls performing useful--and interesting--services.

In library school at Columbia the dream was given historical perspective. "If there were one destination allowed me in a time machine," lectured the American Libraries instructor as he gazed out the window, hands behind his back, "I would choose Philadelphia in October 1876, and I would

1

transport myself to that momentous gathering of library giants
come together to chart the course of our profession.   Lead-
ers in whose footsteps American librarians would walk for
decades, perhaps centuries.   Imagine--Melvil Dewey! William
Frederick Poole! Justin Winsor! Charles A. Cutter! Ains-
worth Rand Spofford! William Thaddeus Peoples!   Can you
imagine the excitement that Friday night at Number 820
Spruce Street in Philadelphia, in the rooms of the Historical
Society, as these titans of the library world converged?"

I imagined.   But library school kept me so busy I
didn't get to test my dream and its new perspective on an
American library all that year.   The summer following grad-
uation I went to Europe and poked my head--or tried to--
into libraries from the British Museum to La Biblioteca
Nazionale Centrale.   But European libraries present ingeni-
ous obstacles to the casual visitor, and often the attempt
was more nightmare than dream fulfilled.

When I returned to the States, it was to work for
that typical American shrine of good reading, the Library
of Congress, and for the next three years most of my library travels were along its 250 miles of shelves or taking
members of the press through its departments in my role as
assistant to the Information Officer.

These were happy years for me, playing my small
part in the great American dream of a well-informed Congress and serving as--yes--as an intermediary between the
great American library and the general public.   The malaise
and doldrums faded away, but not my curiosity as to what
was actually going on out there in Libraryland--a land to
which I had supposedly gained citizenship with my graduate
degree.   In the library literature, I was reading the same
press releases I had received for my LC Information Bulletin:

news of projects and appointments, not descriptions of life
and feelings, if indeed these existed among my colleagues.
I still wondered, was it good to be a librarian in America?

I thought I would come closer to the heartbeat of the
library nation when I took my next post, associate editor of
Wilson Library Bulletin, without losing ground in the enjoy-
able but specialized area of trade journalism I was getting
myself into. Although I had already published a pair of
articles in Library Journal on visiting the libraries of Europe
(I'd seen many more on a second trip), I'd still not written
a word on the library life of my countrypeople. And what
did I know about it? I hadn't even been to a conference!

That last shortcoming was remedied soon enough in
my term at WLB--even before my official starting date--
when I helped cover the 1969 Midwinter Meeting of the American Library Association in Washington. It was my first exposure to American librarians at large, and I was shocked.
Such rushing about, such ranting, such raving--such bitching
--over words in a document, over parliamentary procedure,
over this committee, that committee! I was inundated by
jargon and the dark gloom of the Shoreham Hotel, barely
able to come up gasping for air with the question still on my
lips: Is it good to be a librarian in America?

WLB's staff was small, heroic, and it was very difficult to escape from one's desk in the Bronx except to attend more national conferences. Only once in the first year
did I manage to get out and observe a library in action: a
full day at a suburban school library near Washington, D.C.
I had mixed feeling about what I saw and about how the library's realities lived up to the ideals of the school library
Standards (the report appeared in WLB, April 1969), but
one thing came across so loud and clear that its echoes fol-

lowed me back to the Bronx to keep alive the library dream:
the librarians were doing something of value--and enjoying
it.

My pursuit of the dream was interrupted by the broader concerns of the war.   You remember the war--reformists
from the Congress for Change and elsewhere vs. the library
establishment and its conservative allies.   The time was summer 1969, during the annual American Library Association
conference in Atlantic City, and the confrontation between library left and right was so intense that, during a late night
strategy session at Radical headquarters, I was accused of
being an establishment spy for lurking in the shadows with
notepad and camera.   It was an exciting time, no doubt
about it, and the emergence of so many young and impas-
sioned foot soldiers of the profession--very few of whom had
been at the Midwinter conference--was for me an enormously
encouraging aspect of library life in America.

But most of the action and rhetoric was political--
Vietnam hung heavy in the air--or had to do with structural,
internal reform in ALA, and I learned no more about life as
it is lived at the front lines of library service than I was to
learn at later national conferences.   Understandably, such
conferences give librarians an opportunity to put aside the
particulars that may or may not make their jobs interesting,
and to concentrate either on issues common to the whole
profession or highly specialized interests.   For some, of
course, conferences are an escape from all responsibility
and reality, a week of non-bookish debauchery as sweet and
pure as honey with only an occasional sticky aftermath.   This
purpose, too, is understandable, but led me no further along
in my own quest.

This search of mine was less an overt chase than an

inner compulsion driven partly by my guilt for not being at
the front lines myself.   I needed to understand libraries from
empirical evidence as well as from the concepts taught in library school; I needed answers to the whining and wailing at
conferences and in the library press.

That groaning was getting even louder in my early
years at WLB, for now it reflected not only internal strife
in the profession, but bitterness against the Nixon Administration's screwing of library priorities after the robust Johnson
era.   And the war in Vietnam went on.

It had been a long winter in 1970-71.   Even left-wing
activists in America were slumping, and library reformists
were telling one another that their own movement "had offered little more than rhetoric in the way of concrete alternatives." My imprisonment in the Bronx had been relieved
during the year by such assignments as an Airlie Conference
on Interlibrary Communications and Information Networks--
at which the great American Library Dream was of a universal (computerized) bibliographic web--and coverage of the
latest budget crises of the New York Public, where library
life was in fact death by strangulation.

Spring came.   My own writing was embittered, un-
thawed.   I had to get free!   I seized at the first excuse: a
25th anniversary celebration of the Prince Georges County
(Md.) Memorial Library, featuring the opening of a swank
new branch.   I made the arrangements, and a friend suggested that, as long as I was down that way, why not extend
my trip a few days and see what was going on in grass-roots
West Virginia, than which no roots are grassier.   Stop talking about it and do it! said the friend.

I did it.   What I experienced as a result of that trip
is expressed in Chapter One of this book, which originally

appeared in the June 1971 <u>WLB</u> as "Spring, National Library
Week, and an Observer Come to Small-Town Library, U.S.A.
(W. Va.); Or, Seed Money, Grass Roots, and the Greening of
the American Library Dream. "

The dream.   Yes, I was on its trail at last, hunting
down the evidence that library life in America could be beautiful!   I had no idea that the article would launch a series
when I wrote it, but my own feelings and the correspondence
that began coming in convinced me that I had struck a chord
in the national library consciousness.   It was spring, a time
of rebirth, and my <u>God</u> how we needed some good news,
some reaffirmation of the faith with which we had entered
librarianship: that it's worth doing for its own sake, however
great the struggle.

On the one hand, the timing could not have been better
for tales of heroic American librarians working with very little money and a lot of heart.   The ALA Washington Office
passed out copies to Congressmen, saying it was exactly the
kind of input legislators wanted in order to justify federal
spending.   On the other hand, it was unpopular in my circle
of reformist friends to be overly optimistic, pollyannaish,
lest it lead to tolerance and neglect of persistent wrongs.
Vice President Agnew had brought new dignity in spite of himself to the nattering nabobs of negativism.   In my heart I
knew he was wrong in his defamation of war protestors--but
right in regard to the futility of eternal naysaying, of gloom
and doom and paranoid mistrust and fascist-pig labeling.
Library journalism had been firing away relentlessly at the
easy targets--the establishment, the Fat Cats--and library
journalists had left their offices mainly for closer looks at
the problems of the profession, not its triumphs or everyday
affirmations.

Recently I came across Bill Moyers' <u>Listening to America</u> (1971) in which he tells of the advice he carried with him throughout his much greater odyssey in search of national values. The advice was in the form of a letter from a friend, urging him not "to go out earnestly in search of America's problems but rather in search of its humor, its ironies, its human-ness. Since we are obviously on the frontier of every new and old problem suffered by mankind, we need to be reminded that we are no worse than the rest of the human race. How can the United States ... offer decent leadership unless we can laugh a little and stop our endless self-flagellations?"

I received similar letters after the West Virginia report, and I bore them in mind throughout my other trips around the country. <u>We need to be reminded that librarianship is no worse than the other areas of human endeavor and stop our endless self-flagellations</u>. I don't deny that my journal is slanted toward the positive view--and sometimes a rose-colored view--of library life. There is a very thin line between healthy optimism and pollyannaism, and who can tread it without a misstep now and then? But no fact is intentionally altered, no problem deliberately overlooked to give the illusion of joy or success or satisfaction where there is none. The truth is, damn it, that it <u>is</u> good to be a librarian in America for those actually out there working in a library and not fifteen times removed from public service in a magazine office, faculty lounge, government desk, or some other remote station within the profession. For openers, America <u>is</u> a land of libraries, libraries you can visit as casually as you please, libraries in almost every little town, libraries where you can read what you want, libraries that employ some 100,000 of us and serve some fifty million Americans

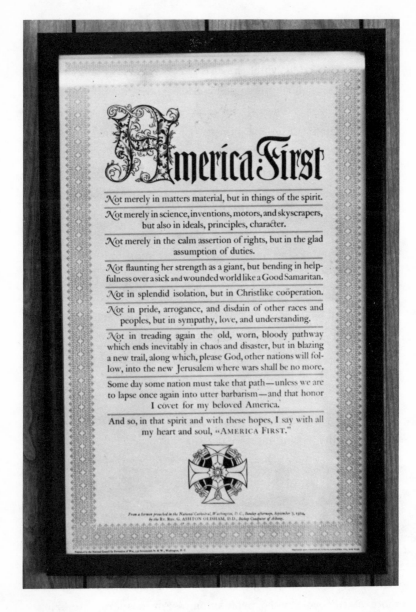

Framed poster in the Altamont, N. Y., Public Library.

directly, all Americans indirectly. Let us never, never take
this basic blessing for granted or without celebration. Sweet
land of libraries, of thee I sing! Then let's go find what's
wrong with them, as well as right, and make them better.

I have hoped that this series has accomplished some
good for others in addition to the rewards it provided for me.
Several librarians of whom I wrote have suggested that it has:

"You see what your ... article did for the Bellevue
Library! Publicity such as this ["Bellevue's 'Dream' Library," p. C-1, Bellevue American] is what we kneel and
pray for nightly." --Lynn Lancaster, Bellevue, Wash.

"Both BARC & SCAN were funded (and funded well, I
thought) for next year. Perhaps your article had something
to do with it!" --Gil McNamee, BARC director.

"Your article has given me a needed boost." --Kevin
Starr, San Francisco City Librarian.

And so on. May it give other readers--librarians in
the field, library school students, prospective librarians, librarians removed from the grass roots--a needed boost in
these hard times.

                                                    A. P.

New York, December 1974

It was spring, and it was National Library Week in an altogether American-looking public library, Marion County, West Virginia.

Chapter One

In the Springtime of the Seventies:

West (ByGod!) Virginia and
That Good Old Mountain Make-Do

It was Earth week! It was Peace week! It was National Library Week! It was Spring! And in gloriously green and floriferous Washington--where the Administration spends more these days to fertilize its lawn than it recommends for public library construction (FY 1972:$0)--President Nixon remarked: "It is appropriate during this week to pay tribute to the repositories of American wisdom and experience and to welcome their exciting part in preparing our citizens to meet better the pressing social challenges of our time."

In New York City, amidst the Springtime fulmination of odoriferous filth, it seemed a good time to leave one's desk at Wilson Library Bulletin for a couple of days, leave the over-observed East Coast Megalopolis altogether for a while, and to seek out a few old-fashioned American towns and their libraries. It was a good time for some old questions to be asked anew:

What is the effect of federal funding on public library services? What does it actually look like, and what does it lead to? (The President's FY 1972 budget represented the third year in a row that the Administration budget drastically reduced or eliminated programs of library aid.)

11

In which areas is even more federal aid required if
libraries are to act in the federal interest; for instance, in
the reduction of educational inequality and of migration away
from rural areas and small towns?

Which shortcomings of library service might not be
remedied magically by increased federal aid?

What is the state of the art at the grass-roots level?
And so, Steinbeck-style, a New York editor struck out to find
the real America and what it was up to, this time in its libraries, driving 1, 200 miles in less than three days (April
18-20) to do so. Of course, when one's time is that abundant, one takes a sampling rather than a survey, and the
sampling chosen here was from deep in the hills of West
Virginia.

Why West (By God!) Virginia? Because of all States
within a day's drive of New York--and in the Nation, for that
matter--the "Mountain State" probably shows most clearly the
difference between on-going library services as supported by
federal (and related State) funds, and floundering or dismally
deprived services that have lacked this support. Consider
that this Appalachian State, many of whose 1, 800, 000 persons
have all the time--and all the need--in the world now for the
services of public libraries (for they are victims of failing
industry), consider that this State ranks last in the country
in per capita support of libraries; ranks in the lowest 10 percent in the number of library books owned (8/10 of a book
per capita); has a total of 35 professional librarians currently employed in the public libraries; and according to the State
Library Commission, needs about 25 new library buildings
to provide equal educational opportunity throughout the State.
Then consider that the President's budget cut would reduce
the total federal allotment to the State from $468, 477 to

$245,492. Library service for half the population would be reduced, with 30 library positions Statewide placed in jeopardy. In addition, hours of public service would be reduced by one-third, and a fourth of the bookmobiles--the educational lifeline to many rural communities--would have shorter schedules, while purchases of library materials would be reduced by $136,000.

Now, speaking of the President, let's make one thing perfectly clear: West Virginia is not the poorest State in the Nation; its library services, at their best, can match those almost anywhere; and its libraries are not the only ones hurting in the face of threatened federal cuts and tight local money--not by a long shot. Just glancing at a few press releases coming through currently, one reads of crises in North Carolina, Oregon, Tennessee, Connecticut, upstate New York, and, as happens every Spring, the New York and Brooklyn public libraries. But areas such as these last have fiscal and social problems of such complexity that it is virtually impossible to identify their effects on any given service, such as libraries. In a place like West Virginia, things are often a little simpler, more suitable for quiet observation, isolated from the hysterical complexities of coastal life in America. One travels 50 miles out of Washington into W. Va.'s Eastern Panhandle, and they ask you: "Are you from back East?" In West Virginia, if the big library trailers the State Library Commission sends out to the sticks are denied federal support, their services will be cut by 50 percent. Cut library services by half to 194,509 people who have precious little access to other self-educational materials --and one can observe deprivation in the hills that might never be noticed in the jungles of the big cities. Or, when a $95,000 library in Calhoun County, built with $75,000

A West Virginia man pauses in front of the Martinsburg-Berkeley County Library, built in 1968 among some controversy. A few citizens didn't think it should have moved from four stuffy rooms in the old City Hall, which can be seen reflected in the glass doors.

in federal funds, is kept going with the proceeds from local
pancake suppers--that's visible, too.

Federal Rape of a Public Square

Not every member of this beautiful and friendly State,
of course, is sold on libraries and their manifestations of
federal aid. In Martinsburg, first stop on the three-day trek,
the manager of the only local radio station goes on the air
regularly to blast the town's Martinsburg-Berkeley County
Library and the $600,000 building it moved to in 1968 from
four stuffy rooms at the top of City Hall. The graceful
brick edifice (which to this observer is a handsome comple-
ment to the classical and Georgian brick structures nearby)
he attacks as a "rape of the public square," and its services
as more than the community needs. The Federal Government, which provided $400,000 of the $600,000 for construction and equipment and contributes to the library's operation-
al expenses, shares the guilt of this rapacious and profligate
imposition upon the citizens of Martinsburg's happy apple valley. But the Government also shares in the following little
bonus: that in this area of 19,000 persons, the library cir-
culated 123,000 volumes last year--a figure almost four
times the size of the collection, and, per capita, about twice
the national average for library book circulation! Further,
that local gifts, not public funds, accounted for the other
$200,000 in building expenses; that townspeople bring in vis-
itors to show off the library as the architectural pride of
Martinsburg; that, as a direct result of the new building,
circulation has doubled over figures prior to 1968; and that,
as a Service Center Library receiving federal cash grants,
it ties in to the State's growing system network--or, in more

human terms, it links people with the resources and information they want, however distant.

More than the community needs? What an insult to
the people of Martinsburg! How can one man presume to set
the limits on another person's means toward intellectual
growth? The group of young schoolgirls gamboling through
the children's department during our visit was all plaid-
skirted, blue-jacketed, giggling, wide-eyed innocence now;
but for what will face them in a few short years--the chal-
lenges and opportunities newly open to them, the problems
and calamities to overcome in a dirty, crowded, still-bar-
baric world--to be ideally prepared, they'd need ten times,
a hundred times, the information available to them in this
modest library. During a stop-off on the way to West Virginia to help celebrate the 25th Anniversary of the Prince
George's County (Md.) Memorial Library, it was noted that
the children of this area, neither very rich nor very poor on
the average, have access to 836,000 volumes in their system,
as well as the latest non-book materials and equipment, not
to mention the millions of items available a few minutes away
in Washington, D.C. Has anyone publicly stated that these
resources--which cost the county one and a half cents out of
each tax dollar--are more than the community needs? Why
are the educational opportunities open to citizens of this county more equal than those available to, say, the people of
Martinsburg?

The answer is not only in terms of large sums of
money. One very wise investment of public funds, for instance, is in the making of a professional librarian who knows
how to utilize what resources are on hand. What's the difference between a non-professional and a professional? What
do they learn in library school? For one thing, they learn

not to sit on their fat collections and wait for the library
user to come to <u>them</u>. Although one can't circulate books
one doesn't have, neither does an increase in the book collection guarantee the intellectual flowering of the populace.
Changing a library from a passive archive to an aggressive,
missionary, active educational institution is a tricky and complicated business, and ought not to be left in the hands of
amateur, shushing, keepers of the crypt. So, legislators--
send a kid to library school. But for the best return on the
people's investment, send a kid who is dedicated to the dream
of educational equality, who will work in areas where he or
she is most needed.

Cheryl Flagg is assistant librarian at the Martinsburg
library, a bright and energetic young woman who, along with
head librarian Anna Shewbridge, has done much to nurture
the shoots of federal seed money in her native West Virginia.
At this writing, she does not have her fifth-year library degree, nor, if one can trust his snap judgment, the sense of
urgency--the need to acquire materials in all media and get
them out, fast and furiously--that is properly acquired in the
best graduate library training. And yet, hers is the kind of
forward-moving personality that could keep moving forward
across the State boundaries into higher-paying jobs unless
there is some provision in her educational program for her
to come back home. Once again, a small investment of federal money is working toward this end: Miss Flagg plans to
attend the University of Maryland Library School under a federal "trainee grant" administered by the W. Va. State Library
Commission.

Cheryl will be back. [1] What she might come back to,
however, is already in doubt. With State funds in shorter
supply than usual and with threats of federal cutbacks, only

essential books are being ordered and hours of opening are
being reduced in a pattern similar to that of so many libraries this season. And--never fear--people will learn not to
need libraries open on Saturdays or nights, not to need library materials, period, if that's really what we want to
teach them. After all, they can always get their information
from Martinsburg's one radio station.

Miracle in Berkeley Springs

People come to this cozy valley town (pop. 1, 100)
seeking miraculous curative powers from the same warm
springs that were favorites of George and Martha Washington.
But when the New York library editor arrived, he found a
miracle of another sort: that the Morgan County Library of
Berkeley Springs is circulating about 12, 000 volumes a year,
is staying open for study and reference about 750 hours a
year, on a total, annual budget of $1, 500!

Amy Catlett is not a professional librarian, but she
is dedicated and efficient in running the warmly furnished,
cheery, one-room county library. She has to be dedicated--
imagine what's left for her out of $1, 500 after $600 goes for
books and some more for maintenance and miscellaneous expenses. Times have been both better and worse in her 14
years at the library, but she's happy with things as they are.
Her book budget she calls a blessing ("I buy everything on
sale"), and her secret weapon in managing the library work-
load is a tall, "yessir, yes'm" 14-year-old named Roger
Moss, who has logged 650 volunteer hours since last summer.
Roger isn't getting rich, but he likes to read, and he's got
5, 000 books around him.

In conjunction with National Library Week, the town

was about to celebrate "Be Kind to Amy Day," and an editorial in The Morgan Messenger had yielded $12 for the li-
brary in just four days! Well, it isn't that the town doesn't
love Amy and her library--according to a local teacher, they
do, they do; but there just isn't much of anything in Berkeley
Springs except friendliness, warm baths, and lovely hills, and
that's the rub--

The Morgan County Library, heroic miracle and labor
of love that it is, is no more what a library ought to be than
Kon-Tiki is any way to cross an ocean. Its furnishings and
equipment for circulating books are up to reasonable standards,
but only because there was some federal money (matched by
local funds) available for this purpose. Otherwise, this library is part of a syndrome that keeps all but a few young
Abraham Lincolns from getting turned on to knowledge outside school or home. As a learning resources center, it's
strictly a books-only, quiet-please, sorry-but-we-do-not-car-
ry-that-sort-of-thing-here operation.

No, we're not going into the bleeding-heart, party-
line rhetoric: how these poor rural have-nots in the world's
richest nation are kept down by the inequities of the Capital-
istic system. There are poverty areas, after all, that make
Berkeley Springs look like Beverly Hills, and who knows if
the Morgan County residents would ever make full use of a
real learning center? But a small incident that occurred
during the visit to this library does seem to have a message
for educators and legislators that's worth a moment's thought
and perhaps a hell of a lot more LSCA services money than
has been recommended:

Two kids came in, about 19 or 20, one of them just
back from the Army, the other a motorcycle freak with
"Born to Raise Hell" tattooed on his arm and a chain around

his boot. The vet could not have been a more perfect repre-
sentation of the young man suddenly faced with a big open
lifetime ahead of him and no special way to start filling it
up. And so he was searching. Looking for some answers
in a little card catalog.

"I used to hang around here a lot," he said. "Now
there's all kinds of books I'd like to get my hands on, but
they just don't have 'em." One of these books was a work
by or about Karl Marx. He'd heard some talk about Marx-
ism, wanted to straighten it out in his head with some of his
ideas about the American way of life, ideas from Army service. Another was Do It! by Jerry Rubin. Rubin, he understood, had advocated killing one's own parents. To the vet,
such a concept was an unspeakable foulness in the gentle
rivers of his West Virginia mind; yet, Rubin was a part of
his age, his history, and he wanted to understand this kind
of thinking.

His friend had a swastika tattooed on his arm along
with the lettering, but now he was looking for another sign.
He said that he was half Cherokee, that he was learning to
be proud of it, and might even head for Coral Gables to try
to live on an Indian Reservation. So he was in this library
for the first time in his life, looking for the proper Indian
symbol to paint on his motorcycle.

It's crazy for one to believe that he just happened to
walk in on a potential turning point in the lives of two young
men. But, as a professional librarian, this writer has to
believe it. A librarian with a decent library or library system could have come up with the desired materials in a hurry and could have used them to pass on to these impression-
able young men the secret of learning: that the world of
knowledge can be entered from any point, and that the key

to the whole business is nothing more than one's own interests.
Idealistic? It does happen in good libraries with librarians
who are trained educators. But it costs more than $1,500
a year.

As for the books and the Indian sign? The library
didn't have them. Sorry. And that was that.

A Proud Library that Begs

The Morgantown Public Library, as an extension-service center, reigns over a mining and industrial kingdom almost twice the size of Luxembourg, a fifth that of Wales,
and is bringer of the book to some 150,000 persons. But
when the Morgantown PL wants to return one of the motion-
picture films it manages to secure from free-loan sources,
it has to go borrow the postage from the Friends of the Library. When the Morgantown PL wanted to paint its so-
called audiovisual room (you can hear a few things there,
but there's usually nothing to see) it had to beg two gallons
from each local paint store, coax a hardware merchant into
mixing them all together properly, and have the paint job
done by the A-V librarian and the cleaning woman. The
Morgantown PL circulates about 350 Talking Books a month
to the blind and physically handicapped; the books come free,
thanks to the Library of Congress and its federal funds, but
the only way they ever got to be kept in some kind of order
was when the library was able to scrounge some shelves from
a local print shop. Federal funds helped get the library out
of its one-room "jailhouse" under a city building and into an
austere but modern two-story structure, but for all four-and-
a-half years that the new building has been occupied, its
basement "dock" has stood empty for want of one bookmobile:

no money for it. Running an extension-service center without a bookmobile in a big, semi-rural area such as Morgantown's is like deep-sea fishing without a boat. Yet somehow,
with a little bit of heroism, a little bit of federal ($16,000),
State ($19,000), and local ($53,000) funding, and a little bit
of help from his Friends, Librarian Elliott R. Horton--with
his staff--manages to do a heap of good in the four-county
service region.

How does he do it? How does he circulate 111,000
volumes annually? Cope with a demand on facilities that now
requires a third floor to be built on top of the library? Provide professional assistance to the far-flung outposts of the
library region?

For one thing, he has paid heroes on his staff, and
volunteer heroes, several from the big University of West
Virginia up the street. One volunteer, in an outreach program for shut-ins, found a 96-year-old woman, abandoned
by her nurse, helpless and untended for longer than one wants
to imagine. The library volunteer helped restore some dignity to her last years. Libraries are more than books being
stamped in and out, you see.

Mr. Horton looks very small when you see him buried
under all his paperwork (things pile up when you have to
spend time begging). But he has a big humanitarian heart
and plenty of courage. Mr. Horton also has good friends
among the local press, gets good ink for the library. He
has friends at the Post Office who will do those extra little
services when he needs them. He has good friends on his
library board, the kind of people who read books, who even
get review copies and pop into his office for a cheery "Good
morning here's a book for the library." He has Junior
Leaguers taking care of the vertical file.

Betty Matheny, roving extension librarian working out of Morgantown, West Virginia, stops along her route to gaze at a mine where disaster took 78 lives in 1968. Her husband is a miner.

There are many things he does not have in his library, in addition to the bookmobile. One of the town's two glass factories is going out of business; money is tighter than usual. So he can't even dream of a young adult collection and program, although the children's program is in good shape, except for non-book materials. He is also short of funds for developing a local history archive--an important function of every public library. There is a local history collection, but no more money for big frills like the local newspaper on microfilm.

For all it does not have, however, the library does have a staff member named Betty Matheny.

Mrs. Matheny, a jolly, hardy, West Virginian, is the roving extension services librarian who pushes her Ford with a vengeance over the treacherous Appalachian hills to make her library rounds. Her salary is paid entirely out of federal funds, but she said "she'd carry on her work for nothing if she had to, but don't quote her"--so forget that last.

Betty Matheny's job is to get the resources and professional know-how of the Morgantown service center out to the virtually-volunteer-operated, store-front libraries of the smaller towns in the area, as well as to the larger libraries dependent on a broader resource base in order to meet their public responsibilities. In addition to plowing through the administrative business at headquarters, she drives endless miles to help out in person, to train local workers, to process materials herself. She's used to hard work; a former teacher who later became a graduate librarian, she used to drive a bookmobile over back-country, mud-and-rut roads that were so bad that half the books fell off their shelves. And today, too, for the time and energy she puts into her job, for the ways in which she touches American lives, she's

one of the best examples you can find of a little federal money
well spent.

Mrs. Matheny also has a quality money can't buy: a
life-long identification with and respect for the people she
serves. Her husband is a miner. She knows something of
the joys, miseries, and aspirations of the thousands of mining families in this coal area. Her husband shares one mis-
ery in particular with them: black lung disease. "It's only
the third stage." she said. There are five stages.

The point is, that when Mrs. Matheny stopped at Con-
sol No. 9 of the Consolidation Coal Company on our way to
a library in Mannington, it was with no pretensions that she
looked out with profound and pensive sadness for the hun-
dredth time over the mine that took 78 lives one day in November 1968.

The mining families are her people, and she wants to
help them in their commitment to the greatest educational
enrichment possible for their children. Farmington, home
of No. 9, has no local library service. There used to be a
bookmobile. Funds ran out.

The storefront library in the little town of Mannington
was started in 1964 with a budget of $25. Mannington, the
richest American town for its size before the oil wells in
back yards ran dry years ago, isn't so rich anymore. Today
the library is the sole branch of the PL of Fairmont, the
nearest city, and gets a $3,000 budget from the county (Mar-
ion). The success of this library--which has a per capita
circulation (12) equal to one we were raving about recently
in Scarsdale, N.Y.--is another story of heroism, dedication,
and a few federal pennies on the one hand, and educational
inadequacy, the need for reasonable LSCA funds on the other.

The catalog of the Mannington, West Va., Public Library.
It isn't much, but in 1963 there was no library and certainly
no place in Mannington to find, say, Catcher in the Rye in
large print.

The local heroine is Charlotte Murphy, an outgoing
auntie type whom the children obviously adore. She keeps
the library open six days a week and plunders the county
treasury of about $1 an hour for her services. Volunteer
aides help her with the busy-work, the Women's Club--which
doubles as the Library Board--provides luxuries like a small
bulletin board and some moral support, and Mrs. Matheny
visits from Morgantown to give on-the-spot professional training and service.

So Mrs. Murphy does a praiseworthy job. Her weekly
international exhibit on one wall is big news among Mannington small fry. Her clients come from all economic levels.

But her budget is still $3,000 in an area of 3,500
persons, and you can't look for educational excellence at
these bargain prices. The library has no phone. Its card
catalog is a precarious pile of metal file drawers. And the
tiny library rooms get so packed with kids that there's a sign
posted: "Please limit your stay to five minutes."

The evening rush hour at Mannington's main intersec-
tion was over in about 12 seconds, and, to a New Yorker, it
looked like a pantomime of people going nowhere in a hurry.
As for the citizens of Mannington--if LSCA funds for a larger
library don't come through, if the children must continue to
pantomime in their five-minute time limit the library enrichment children receive in other American communities--they
could begin to get that same, nowhere feeling.

Last Stop in Grafton

If you missed the last train out of Grafton, you might
have unexpected trouble leaving this smudgy hillside town of
7,400; because even though Grafton probably has more rail-

road tracks than anything else, its rail passenger service is
the latest of the community's life-giving forces to wither
away.

Grafton is a town full of heroes. In 1960, it received
national honors for pulling itself up by the bootstraps after
one of its major industries had moved out. But now even
the bootstraps are worn, and if any town ever needed the kind
of uplifting local pride that a good library can provide--not
to mention its educational values--it's this one.

What Grafton does have is the Taylor County (pop.
18, 500) Public Library, a storefront operation with a total
budget of $1, 500--that dismal figure again.

Once more, local heroism, seeded by grass-roots federal funds, has at least made something out of nothing. Federal funds paid for the pleasant modern furnishings in a re-
furbished store, which replaced a dingy if historic room in
the old Mother's Day Church, to which library patrons practically never came. Federal money, of course, also pays
for the extension services and visits of Mrs. Matheny. In
return, Grafton now has a pleasant, air-conditioned reading
room, a collection of about 9, 000 volumes, a story hour
drawing about 30 children every Saturday morning. Among
the heroes responsible are Russell Walls, local school librarian and library board president, who took a busman's
holiday from his work to raise money for the refurbishing;
Marguerite Baugh, a local woman who operates the library
as best she can for as little as one can possibly be paid; and
such volunteer workers as board member and former teacher
Virginia Hanway, who at least stamps books in and out on
some evenings.

The library is not reaching out to the people. Outreach requires money and professional skill. The kind of

outreach in a shoestring operation like Grafton is a window
display of a set of encyclopedias. The blue bunting used to
set off the books was borrowed from a Kennedy memorial in
the local school.

All We Are Asking

Mr. President, Congressmen, Legislators, City Fath-
ers, Fellow Librarians, and Citizens: with your help libraries have come a long way in the last few decades. But
the library is a changing institution, and its statistics--not
to mention the standards of the American Library Association
--can be extremely confusing in measuring the real effect of
expanded and upgraded library service to the American people
--or the real problems of inadequate service. The attempt
here has been to present a few concrete images, a clear-cut
sampling, for the aid of those who must make unenviable and
excruciating decisions in the allotment of limited funds.

Because many libraries are now at the edge of disaster, their need for continued seed and incentive money at
a reasonable level is an urgent one. Perhaps there are more
urgent crises with a higher priority for available funds, just
as surely as there are wasteful programs that will continue
to receive full funding. Looking ahead, many librarians fear
that a revenue-sharing plan would shortchange such heroic
ongoing programs as those of the West Virginia Library Commission in favor of programs with even more visible--if less
enriching--results. And it is, after all, a lot to ask of bud-
get-makers that they provide money not only for services,
but for the advertisement of those services. For without
dynamic and aggressive outreach, without professionally
guided promotion of the library's recourses, the taxpayers'

money is one-half wasted.

But when library service _is_ properly funded, _is_ known to the public, _is_ used, consider the end result: a people who can choose wisely from the alternatives of life, because, whatever the inadequacies of their schooling, they have discovered all the alternatives through the resources of their library.   That end result is called Freedom; and as they say, what price?[2]

Chapter Two

Trusty Cornhuskers at the
Gateway to the Western Frontier

Wahoo, we were free again! Free, and in a library, half-
way across the country in Wahoo, Nebraska, pop. 3,800.
Through a Conestoga covered wagon etched on the glass door
of the Wahoo Public, we were watching Old Glory flap in a
warm October breeze across the street, a sweet Czech Ko-
lachi in our belly, and feeling good.

Freedom isn't absolute. One is free only from something. For us it was freedom from the East-Coast urban
perspective of life so limiting to New York library journalists.
Even if--as almost happened after Wahoo--we had been jailed
on the Winnebago Indian Reservation for taking pictures of a
library van, we would have still found some solace in our
altered perspective on American librarianship.

For it truly is another world, library life in Frontier-
land, as opposed to the perennial struggles of libraries in
the Metropolitan corridors. Perhaps you have to be a city-
bred Easterner to marvel at some of the distinctions. For
one thing, it looks so different. You step out of the show-
case school library of the Omaha area, and you're in a corn-
field as endless and eternal as the lapis lazuli sky above.
You visit a regional librarian at home, and your gaze travels
from a bookcase filled with Bowker and Wilson imprints, out

31

"Wahoo, we were free again! Free, and in a library, half-
way across the country in Wahoo, Nebraska, pop. 3,800 ...
looking out through the Conestoga covered wagon etched on
the glass door of Wahoo Public...."

the window, to a 320-acre ranch surrounding the house like
an ocean, with some chestnut brown cattle far out in that
golden autumn sea.   You see the hand of Carnegie still in
many little towns, a classical grey temple immutably fixed
against the wide open spaces.   Inside the libraries, your
eyes soon find the ubiquitous stars and stripes--not on seat-
patches or socks, belts and motorcycle helmets, but on--of
all things!--the American flag.   (The Nebraskans are not
blind patriots by any means; but if you've got it, flaunt it--
and they've got a beautiful chunk of America, right in the
heart of the continent, with plenty of space for everyone, the
way it used to be, the way they like it: lots of churches,
clean air, strong families, decent cities, hardworking immigrants, thick steaks, cheap living, God-fearing librarians.
Why not fly the colors?)

Something else looks and sounds different.   Wherever
you go, the spirit of a championship football team haunts you.
Go Big Red!   That slogan!   Nebraskans eat, pray, and even
read by it in the library.   It refers, of course, to the University of Nebraska Cornhuskers, the Big Red, who, as we
were almost getting arrested at Winnebago, were busy winning
their 17th game in a row to keep them ranked number one
among the nation's collegiate football teams for the fall 1971
season.   The State Library Commission has wisely created
a bumper sticker in bright red and white that says:

Go Big--READ
a message from your Nebraska Library

But you don't see as many of these as you do the original
Big Red slogan, which can always be observed within a book's
throw of the libraries, on gas stations, banks, supermarkets,
autos, sweatshirts, and marquees.   And if you don't see

the red slogan, you'll be sure to see another message: "We're Number One!"

Nebraskans and most Middle Americans have a real thing about that number-one business--a neurosis probably induced by years of football rankings and one that has perhaps caused more feelings of insecurity than anything else. There's only one number one at a time, after all. At its worst extreme, President Nixon used the term as a rationalization for further American deaths in Vietnam--to keep America number one; but Nebraskans have at least recognized the superficiality of victory on the field and are heard to ask one another questions such as, "What are those two other things we're number one in again?" Also, the slogan is employed to benefit such humanistic ends as library service. "Any time you say 'number one,'" a leading public librarian in Lincoln told us, "the people respond." Thus, when the University of Nebraska's Don L. Love Library ran a special Homecoming Day fund-raising campaign, it used the slogan, "Make Love (Library) Number One!"--and the students responded by giving up their traditional homecoming floats and donating to the library the money they would have spent on them.

Where Past Meets Present

Nebraska had its centennial of Statehood only five years ago, and its colorful past--woolly pioneer days, Indian life, Union Pacific trailblazing--is still prized everywhere. Two rummage sales on Saturday morning in Wahoo--one in a church, the other in a meeting hall--found scores of townsfolk picking lovingly through the relics of territorial and early Statehood days: through another generation's junk, and this day's treasure.

But down the street, the public library held something just as important to them: the relics of man's intellectual and creative history, as recorded mainly in his books. In pioneer country, where nothing is taken for granted, schools and libraries, learning and learning resources, are cherished and maintained often at considerable sacrifice. For Nebraska has a few millionaires, but the rest of its wealth is spread out pretty thinly over its 77,000 square miles. In our own brief travels in Eastern Nebraska, we came across little red schoolhouses still standing monumentally, and towns with public library service 100 years old.

Nebraskans love their past, all right, but they are neither locked into it nor do they always fear the presence of modern ideas. Their best new libraries--thanks largely to Federal funds carefully spent--are as architecturally au courant as those anywhere; and as a result of those same funds, modern hardware for learning is accessible in most regions, and any book in the country can be requested through TWX centers and interlibrary loan. Most important, however, books representing a broad spectrum of political opinion and social mores were observed on open shelves in the local libraries. It is true that many Nebraska parents would just as soon blockade any East or West Coast imports threatening the status quo. But for the sake of their children, they usually don't. Too many talented and bright young Nebraskans--Karl Shapiro, Willa Cather, Wright Morris, and Dick Cavett, for example--go away or make good elsewhere. Now the idea is to build local pride without stifling freedom of expression. Make it a good place to come back to. One university librarian, known as a conservative to former colleagues in Washington, D.C., is considered a liberal back in his native Nebraska and enjoys the role without persecution.

And, although Nebraskans will sometimes draw the line when
road shows like a gay librarian and his husband play the University lecture hall, book collections have been pretty much
left alone. We talked to dozens of librarians from all areas
and specialities, and not one felt that library censorship was
a particular problem in Nebraska. Several, however, admitted that if ever a book's purchase became a cause célèbre
--as had the showing of the skin flick The Stewardesses in
Omaha--the latent forces of censorship could be devastating.

What are the major problems of Cornhusker librarians?
Aside from the frequent lack of local money to support the
kind of programs that the State and Federal agencies have
seeded and would like to keep going, it's hard to say. One
problem they do not seem to share with librarians of urban
America is that of low morale. Into a State without a single
library school, graduate librarians have come or returned
with the conviction that there is good to be done through libraries and they can do it. The many small-library directors
without degrees are equally committed and confident. It
wasn't so long ago that Nebraskans, with nothing but wind-
torn grass around them, raised up trees and houses and
farms, whole towns and cities. Why shouldn't a spirit of
optimism prevail in all endeavors? As for the relevance of
libraries--never does one hear the disparaging and despair-
ing indictment: "Nothing but a lily-white, middle-class institution!" For what else would you have in a white, middle-
class, Nebraskan town?

There are some exceptions, which are discussed later.
But in general, the main problems have to do with the geo-
graphical remoteness and isolation of some libraries, the
need to make modern services better known, and a great un-
evenness of facilities and resources from town to town. But

these are wholesome problems. The most gruesome tribula-
tion we heard, of those peculiar to Nebraska librarians, was
one told to us by the head of reference for the State Library
Commission: as she drove to work through the fields and
farms surrounding Lincoln, a pheasant smashed neatly through
her windshield and on to the front seat. Otherwise, most
Nebraska librarians will tell you that library work is a pretty clean business. And a noble one.

One can imagine what must be considerable shock and
confusion when some of these librarians attend their first
ALA national conference and hear at the membership meetings the rhetoric of the street, of anarchy, of culpa, and de-
feat. "Libraries are irrelevant to the Gay People! Libraries
are fascist, establishment, rip-offs! Librarians are fat cats!
Racist pigs! Tools! Off the libraries! Burn them down!"

Of course, not even Nebraska is invulnerable to changing times, and its librarians had a chance to hear some fairly funky rhetoric right in their own back yard when Ernie
Chambers, the only black Nebraska State Legislator, socked
it to about seventy-five during the State library association
conference (covered more fully below) that we attended in
Omaha. Some of the librarians--not used to the zingers of
guilt that Easterners have learned to parry lest they be bled
dry--were, as they say, visibly shaken. But Mr. Chambers,
born and educated in Nebraska, addressed himself to all librarians, not just those of his State or those in the room,
who were there because they were forming a new institutional
and social responsibilities section. Speaking extemporaneous-
ly--and very beautifully and forcefully--the young, angry, T-
shirted legislator told all librarians:

"Each man's death diminishes us--but does a mental
death diminish us at all, or is it only when the body ceases

to live? ... Is it all right that a black student can be gradu-
ated from a black high school and not be able to read? ...
You librarians, with the repositories of <u>all</u> man's knowledge
--why are <u>you</u> not the force that electrifies society? You
know the stereotype people have of you! ... I would die and
go to hell ten times before I'd let anyone destroy my child....
You are spineless, anemic, too timid ... to be activists....
There hasn't been one ripple out of you...."

It seemed an unfair generalization to this listener,
who had seen many a library ripple--a preoccupation with
activism, East and West. But Chambers' image of librarians
was formed in Nebraska; and the library group he addressed
was, after all, the <u>first</u> in the 73-year-old Nebraska LA with
any expressed interest in social activism as it is understood
today.

But does that mean that Nebraska's librarians are
afraid to get their hands dirty? Are they all square? Apathetic? Out of it? If raw social change has reached the
Gateway to the West, who are the librarians that must deal
with it? What are they like?

The Beautiful and the Beefy

Of course you can't generalize about people; but being
human, we began to perceive Nebraska librarians as either
the beautiful--those clear-eyed frontiersmen with their graceful, flared nostrils and farm-hardened limbs--and the "beefy,"
as one local librarian herself put it. You can go to beef
fast in this country--mainly from eating too much of it because it's the best in the world--and a lot of folk do.

Nebraskan hair is kept short--many of the library women wear what looks like a freeze-dried bouffant--the spec-

tacles are horn-rimmed, the skirts are long, the suits a size
too large. Even the college and university librarians--those
mavericks--don't break these rules very often. But within
the costume, you might find any kind of player from reactionary to avant garde--although rarely a radical. Two grand-
motherly librarians sat in the back of our car during one
side trip from the conference. From appearances, you could
never have told which was the "urban" school librarian and
which the small-town public librarian; but when they started
talking about library service to youngsters, they could not
have been more different. The school librarian's rap was
rich with images of discovery, of freedom, of self-determina-
tion for her students, of room and encouragement for them
to spread their wings; the public librarian spoke of restric-
tions, of enforced silence, of guarding her books against the
mischief of the town's youngsters. She got on the subject of
crime and criminals: lock them up for good, she told us.

The public librarian was an "Out-Stater," which means
anyone not from Omaha or Lincoln; but one could not attribute
her attitudes to this characteristic any more than to her status
as a rural public librarian. Both reactionary and progressive
spirits were to be found in every area of library life in Nebraska.

But we did single out one characteristic shared by almost all the librarians we met--one that will play an important part in the future of library services in Middle America:
trust. Trust of one another, trust in human nature, trust in
authority, and in the future--something long gone in the population centers of the nation.

We talked at length about this quality to someone who
deals with thousands of area librarians in the course of his
work: a "representative" of a large Midwestern library ser-

vices firm.   That's right--a salesman!   No kidding, in Nebraska you talk to them as if they were human, as if they
weren't out to get you in one way or another for a lousy buck.
As if they were exhibitors of something potentially useful,
not exhibitionists of the commercially obscene.   Imagine?
At the first general session of the conference, the full corps
of exhibitors was paraded across the front of the room and
praised to the sky, and each representative was introduced
to the audience.   Is that trust?

        "Yes," said the rep we talked to.   "Librarians know
they're not going to get screwed by regional salesmen because they rarely do.   So they trust us.   And you can't hard-
sell the people here.   They'll back right off."   Himself a
native of a town of a thousand in Iowa, he admitted that it
helps if one is from the local area.   "But I'm afraid that
even a slick operator from the East could make a killing here
before they stopped trusting him.

        "But you know," he mused, "it's _fun_ to work with
these people.   It's almost a treat for them to get a service
visit.   They don't think of it as a sales call."

        We encountered this trust everywhere in Nebraska life.
Nobody locks anything.   Cigar boxes with petty cash stand un-
attended on counters; you make your own change.   Librarians
were generally shy of our camera and notebook, but not one
objected to being photographed or interviewed--which happens
to us elsewhere, to be sure.   The only instance of mistrust
was at the Winnebago Reservation, discussed later, but then,
why should Indians anywhere trust Great White Library Journalist?

        Trust is exactly what is necessary if Nebraska librar-
ies are to overcome their remoteness and their isolation
from resources for changing times.   They need to cooperate.

They need to hook into systems.   In the metropolitan areas
of the country, interlibrary cooperation may be more a game
of librarians than a demand of users, which is why untrusting libraries have been able to refuse to cooperate or drop
out of systems without a peep from their patrons, who may
have more resources than they use already.   But in Nebraska,
where 229 of the State's 261 public libraries serve communities of less than 5,000, if your local library doesn't have it
--where do you go?   In the next decade, the State Library
Commission hopes to coordinate the development of six multi-
regional networks giving local service through union listings,
centralized processing, cooperation between all types of libraries and other agencies, professional staffing at the centers, common borrowers' cards, and telephone and TWX requests.   You don't bring about these developments without
trust.   Nebraska librarians have been trusting so far.   But
will it hold up?[3]

First, they will have to trust their youthful new Nebraska Library Commissioner, Robert E. Kemper, who was
brought from his library school teaching post at the University of Oregon to coordinate the new cooperative movement.

Kemper's doctoral work concerned cooperation between
people, and, although he seems knowledgeable in human en-
gineering, in behaviorism, he sounds a good deal more humanistic than most of that bunch.   At Eugene, for instance,
he taught cataloging as the cataloging of people, not documents
--as helping one group of people find the people who have
written information for them.   He looks trustworthy--solid
build, innocent Colorado-bred, Kansas-fed smile, an air
about him that goes well with the open Nebraska landscape--
and he works hard.   But even if they accept his leadership,
Nebraska librarians are not about to be herded as easily as

Robert E. Kemper didn't come from Nebraska, but during his term as State Library Commissioner he seemed to fit right in with the land.

the cattle some of them raise into anything they don't like.

"You can easily get cooperation involving machines--
TWX, computers, and so on," Kemper told us as we lit into
some of that Nebraska beef in Omaha, "but to get people to
cooperate with people--that's another story. You can find
that suddenly old friends won't even say hello to each other."

We saw evidence of the theory here and there. For
instance, one small library was suddenly told by its regional
headquarters that no telephone or TWX requests were to be
sent later than noon. Since the library didn't even open until that time, it was the end of system borrowing for the people of that community. A representative from the State Commission was looking into it.

But Nebraskans are human, after all, and there are
always exceptions, always extremes. At a banquet table during the conference, we observed one native Nebraskan public
librarian so untrusting of a State Commission librarian across
from her that she would accept no opinion on any subject.
"Are you from Nebraska?" she asked the State librarian during a discussion of Lincoln's medical facilities. "No? Well
then that's the kind of attitude I'd expect from you." She
discounted the importance of health services. "The sooner
people realize that we're only on this earth for a short trial,
the better off we'll be." It made one reluctant to comtem-
plate her attitude toward library service.

Another extreme is found in those librarians who are
so taken with the brightness of the future they they sometimes
view the present with rose-colored glasses, a shield against
the glare of their own optimism. When we dared to suggest
to the librarians of a city system that they might be closing
some old Carnegie branches faster than the local clientele
wanted to switch to the spiffy new locations--why we were

blitzed by a defense that would have challenged the Big Red!
"This library is not about to abandon any part of this community!" we were told, so don't you give us any of that Library Journal kind of muckraking.

    We didn't have time to check out the neighborhood peo-
ple, but, whatever their feelings, it would have been very
difficult for them to overcome the momentum of the system's
rosy "progress."

    The first three librarians we ran into during an un-
announced visit to the Omaha Public Library displayed an interesting range of attitudes. "Is there any censorship in this
library?" we asked. "No," said Number One. "No," said
Number Two. But the third: "Yes." He admitted, however,
that it wasn't so bad. The library has Do It! and Steal This
Book, but not The Sensuous Man. Had the mayor of Omaha
ever been in the library, there might have been more problems. But he's never stopped by.

    "Are there black ghettos in Omaha?" we asked. "No,"
said One. "No," said Two. "Yes," said Number Three,
who has lived in what he considers a ghetto in North Omaha
for four years, first because it was cheap, but now because
he has many friends there. Intelligent, idealistic, Bob Flood,
the third librarian, represents good young blood for the Omaha Public. That he can work as a Librarian I with only a
bachelor's degree is to the library's benefit. (He will need
to go out of State for a master's in librarianship, which will
make him eligible for promotions.) Like all libraries, Omaha can stand to have a little racial consciousness-raising imposed on them now and then. There are relatively so few
blacks in Nebraska that the need for library materials and
facilities to serve them is not always visible. But in spite
of a 76-year-old main building that looks like something

dredged up from a Venetian canal, the Omaha Public Library
is moving reasonably well into modern times.

And so the variety of people working in Nebraskan libraries is considerable. Perhaps the best generalization one
could make about them, even more than that they are trust-
ful, is that they are in libraries out of love for the work.
Because as Rose Zumpfe, librarian of the Crete Public,
summed it up: "It is not a job at which one gets rich."
And if low pay weren't proof enough of the librarians' enjoy-
ment of the work, then one could consider the long hours of
volunteer duty that many library workers throw in. The assistant head of the Lincoln Public Library puts in about four-
teen hours daily and hasn't taken a work day off in three
years. Half-time employees at the State Commission have
a way of looking like full-time workers. Louise B. Shelledy,
on a one-quarter-time line as executive secretary of the Nebraska Library Association, when cited for her full-time dedication, remarked: "I seen my duty and I done it." The
malady is contagious: Richard Bailey, a partner in a Lincoln public relations firm, has become practically a full-
time friend of Nebraska libraries--far in excess of what
would be expected for the small jobs his firm does for them.
These slim pickings have already been repaid by an estimated
quarter-million dollars of free air time promoting libraries
that young Bailey secured. But you can tell just from the
quality of the work he does for them that he's no false friend
--there is love in it.

NLA--The Living, Dead, and Unborn

"Civilization is a partnership between the living, the
dead, and the yet to be born," said Frank Wardlaw, editor

of the University of Texas Press. "Libraries are essential
if this partnership is to exist." He was addressing an awards
dinner at the 73rd Annual Nebraska Library Convention, held
Oct. 21-22 in Omaha. Have you ever been to a Nebraska
library conference? Well, folks, it's pretty much like any
other State conference, about equally divided between living,
dead, and yet-to-be-born ideas.

There's nothing dead or constrictive about Omaha itself, with its busy, mile-wide streets and mountainous buildings. Why, four-tone men's shoes were in the windows, female impersonators were in the San Moritz, and the Filthy
Follies were headlining at the Cheetah Lounge. So a New
Yorker felt right at home outside the plastic-posh Hilton.
Inside the conference hotel, however, we ran smack into a
historical Nebraska display and never, throughout the meetings,
lost that Cornhusker's sense of place: Nebraska this, Nebraska that.

We chatted with a school librarian before the meetings
began. Eunice Parrish of the Tecumseh Public School is
head of the NLA's School, Children's and Young People Section, but that doesn't make her top anything in Nebraska; too
many of the school librarians have organizational allegiance
elsewhere, such as the Nebraska Educational Media Association. But Mrs. Parrish chatted wisely about school libraries
and her own community of 2,058. About half her school kids
are from farms, but they are generally "liberated" from the
limitations of agricultural interests. There is one black
child--"in a foster situation"--and, reportedly, he's having
a ball in the library. So is the librarian, a native Nebraskan, except when budget time rolls around--when funds for
items like AV hardware are nowhere to be found. (A little
later, we visited the "showplace" Millard School Library out-

side Omaha. "Where is your media center?" we asked one
of the school's thousand teenagers when we arrived at the
sleek new building. "I don't know," she said, "but the library's that-a-way." The library facility was posh, but
there was neither the kind nor amount of materials on the
shelves and tables necessary to create an appealing educational environment. Only two or three students were motivated
to browse there after school hours.)

We found a few librarian mavericks strolling about
before the conference meetings, but in this case they were
only some shy members of the UNO (University of Nebraska
at Omaha) community, where the football team is nicknamed
the "Mavericks." Next to the Big Red of UNL, the Omaha
gridders suffer inescapably from an inferiority complex--and
probably more than that: "I've never seen a football player
in the library," said one of UNO's shy librarians.

Shyness is another generalization one is tempted to
make about Nebraska librarians. At the first general session, a score of them crowded uncomfortably at the door to
watch the proceedings rather than occupy seats in nearby
rows. But this sort of thing happens at most library conferences. At this session, San Francisco Librarian John Anderson addressed his topic of "Our Libraries, Today and Tomorrow, and Other Platitudes," and then added a few platitudes of his own (albeit, some worthy ones): "Get out on the
street as missionaries." "We are lousy communicators."
"Our main question is, 'Who is the user?'" He told how
San Francisco had just spent $80,000 for market research
on the user--and had found out that they needed to find out a
lot more.

The Nebraskans blinked. The sum was half the total
annual budget of their State Library Commission. No wonder

Kemper (Commission director) at the Public Library Section
meeting could speak authoritatively on accountability; a lot is
expected of him for that sum.   He emphasized that results
are accomplished only through a whole chain of cooperating
individuals, beginning with the patron.   "The Congressman
wants to know, " he said, "what, after $15 million has been
spent, are the library patrons doing now that they weren't
doing before?" The Commission is now working on a five-
year plan that must be completed by June 30 and which will
define accountable goals to achieve with Federal and State
funds.

The morning of the business meeting we talked to a
University of Nebraska at Lincoln librarian whose hair was
a little longer than his colleagues'.   We called him the Token
Radical, but he was simply a gentle and responsible young
man with a social consciousness who was a little worried
about the ability of Nebraska librarians to overcome compla-
cency, hit-and-run paternalism, and other pitfalls as the
library-activist movement seeped in from East and West.
Even some young Nebraska librarians, we observed, are so
nervous about power-to-the-people politics that the new social
responsibilities round table formed at the conference eschewed
any such nomenclature or association with ALA's SRRT.   The
thirty gathered together called themselves the Special and Institutional Libraries Section and talked only about services
to the blind and physically handicapped and to prisoners.
For these purposes, however, it was a good show of enthusiasm and a hopeful development.

If you grew up at ALA annual business meetings, you
generally associate the term business with blistering bombast
and even some talk of burning and bombing.   There was nothing like that at NLA's business meeting, which was attended

by about 200 of the association's record 732 membership.
Some solid developments were reported, such as legislation
being introduced for the Library Commission to become a
depository for State documents and publisher of a checklist;
a handbook in the works on intellectual freedom was returned
to committee; and some "hot" announcements were made by
President Kathlyn King Lundgren, at least one of them, like
the Williams & Wilkins/NLM copyright suit, more than three
years old.

        We go to too many conferences, perhaps. After a
while, all business meetings begin to sound to us like whis-
perings of the dead, a slavering drone of jargon and clichés
babbled in self-torment by lost souls in limbo. (Into which
circle would Dante place librarians whose monologues are as
warmed-over cabbage?) But a refreshing rebirth, a reju-
venating burst of living spirit, came to us in the nick of
time from a 90-year-old Nebraskan who was guest of honor
at the NLA Awards Banquet: John J. Neihardt, beloved Nebraska Poet Laureate.

        Mr. Neihardt was there to receive the association's
first Mari Sandoz Award, and both writers instill such in-
credible pride in the hearts of Nebraskans that their names
are usually spoken in a semi-swoon. When Neihardt appeared
on the Dick Cavett show, which reaches Nebraska at 10:30 p.m.
their time, he drew one of the biggest responses of all time
from the national audience. One Nebraskan librarian told us,
"It was the only time I ever stayed up late enough to watch
Cavett."

        The small, white-maned poet, lecturer, and scholar of
Indian philosophy and religion recited--sang--some of his po-
ems, and you could hear the sighs when he expressed his
hope of dying as "a fiddle string/that hears the master's

melody/and snaps. "

Neihardt told the happy librarians that he would treasure the Sandoz award and keep it among those he is saving for old age.

And so, the dead revived by the living, we left the conference with a good feeling and headed toward a ceremony of "the yet unborn" downstate in Lincoln.

Dedicated Lincolnites at a Dedication

On Sunday, October 24, we attended the dedication of the beautiful new Victor E. Anderson Branch Library of the Lincoln Public Library; a week earlier, another new branch had been dedicated. Lincolnites had voted a total of $860,000, for the two libraries in a bond issue, and they showed up by the hundreds to see the ceremonial birth of each new child. The whole event was a marvelous symbol of modern Middle America. First of all, the libraries had been designed to replace two classic old Carnegie buildings, symbols of American public librarianship for as long as anyone can remember. All Carnegie buildings were given outright, of course, with the condition that the town provide land and a yearly operational budget equal to the cost of the structure. Lincoln PL Director Charles E. Dalrymple checked with the Carnegie Corporation people before he went ahead with his plans, and Carnegie decreed that, yes, the buildings had served their original function, go ahead and tear them down. And so two little temples of nostalgia will eventually give way to modernization and expansion, which is so very American. Not everyone in Lincoln is crazy about the idea, especially those living near the old branches. But dissent giving way to the will of the majority isn't so strange to Americans, either. The new

buildings themselves, constructed with an open space concept
with few interior walls and much window glass, reflect the
openness of the Heartlands very nicely. And at the Anderson
branch dedication ceremony, Lincoln's Middle Americans heard
the board president give 20 minutes of credits--flag by American Legion, etc.; the mayor came forth in chortling good
humor; U.S. Representative Charles Thone grasped constituent
arms and shoulders; and the citizens milled about in reverent
delight over their newest possession, although not quite sure
what to do at a library opening other than flip through diction-
aries and atlases.

If there is a slight tone of cynicism here, it is only
because the temper of the times makes it impossible to write
reverently about USIS-style Americana. But Lincoln was a
positive experience, all told. And if there is political power
behind the growth of the city's libraries--well, hooray for us!
Assistant City Librarian Dick Ostrander, dynamo and former
New Jerseyite, said he wouldn't go back East for a million
bucks. "There's just as much pressure here," he told us,
"but there's more that you can get done. A lot of young library people are involved. It's less frustrating. You see
results faster."

It sounded good, and for Lincoln, which has dough,
it is very probably true. But before we returned to New
York, we wanted to look around for ourselves, up and down
the eastern edge of the State, to get a feeling about how others were getting things done.

A Lightning Library Trek Outstate

Everyone writes about the yellow-green cottonwood
trees running along the streams through infinite Nebraska

fields of grain. But seeing it, feeling its beauty, is probably
the only way for a New Yorker to understand why Nebraska
librarians brave the freezing winters, the chilling isolation,
the cultural emptiness of Outstate just to enrich a few souls
with the offerings of their modest libraries. The message of
the cottonwoods is, perhaps, that what is most beautiful is
not profusion, but a spare oasis appearing out of virtual emptiness; and intellectually, in some of the places we visited,
the library is just that oasis.

   In Wahoo, described earlier, the library has been a-
round for 60 years. Its new building is warm, carpeted, inviting; bright new books and other materials are displayed
everywhere. Its collection supplements those of two school
libraries and circulates at the rate of 150 to 200 items a day
--well above the national per-capita average. New materials
have already created a space problem, and yet they add to
the oasis-like environment, the richness, available here for
the small community.

   At Crete, a town of 4,444 in the southeast of the
State, the library is in an old brick Carnegie building, packed
to the rafters with old and new materials, and again, is one
of the oases in a town dominated by the most enormous grain
elevators ever to loom over a small main street. Here, in
this Czechoslovakian community where an old-country respect
for learning has carried over, there are also substantial
school library collections for children. But Librarian Rose
Zumpfe has practically a free hand in choosing materials for
the public library, and she does not hesitate to incorporate
those that tell of an America very different from what was
going on outside the day we visited: it was Veteran's Day,
and there were so many flags flying, so many cub scouts
running around, canons going off, and patriots standing tall,

Rose Zumpfe, Czechoslovakian-born librarian of the predominantly Czech-American community of Crete, Nebraska.

it looked like a scene from Music Man. Protestors would
have been decidedly unwelcome.

Mrs. Zumpfe had let us into the library, but it was
not open to the public on this holiday.

"I started to open," she said, "but everyone thought
it would be unpatriotic."

The skillful and self-taught librarian of Crete came
from Czechoslovakia when she was ten, and has an easy and
natural charm about her that has probably helped her to maintain control of her collection if not always the library hours.

"One man does come in twice a year to censor," she
told us.

"What happens?"

"Nothing," she said modestly. Then she grinned, and
allowed herself what is probably a very rare indulgence in
pride.

The oases nurtured in the open spaces by the traveling regional librarians are even more dramatic. An outreach
program on Nebraska's Winnebago Indian Reservation, for instance, has been set up by a librarian responsible for a bi-
State regional project and run by Winnebagos. The librarian,
Marie Jones of the Sioux City (Iowa) Public Library, arranged
with the tribal authorities on the reservation for us to visit,
but some wires crossed, and we were unable to enter the
church in which the library was housed. Even our look at
the traveling library van parked outside was cut short. There
are intra-tribal hostilities arising from differences between
militant young Indians and the Bureau of Indian Affairs sup-
porters, whom the militants call Apples (red outside, white
inside), and suspicions of strangers run high. As we were
taking a few pictures and talking to the Winnebago library
aides, a redneck trooper with two guns approached us and

Edith Casaday of the Winnebago Tribe describes her frustrations as a community leader for Iowa and Nebraska Winnebagos and her experiences as a library aide in the Sioux City Indian Center collection of the Public Library.

advised us: "Move out or you're goin' to jail." We glanced
at a concrete outhouse across the street that was marked
JAIL in crude letters, and we moved out smartly. Nothing
in library school had prepared us to do otherwise.

But we were there long enough to perceive that the
reservation is no Happy Hunting Ground. Outside the spare
homes of the Indians and the spiritual institutions that sustain
them, the reservation is a cluster of broken-down nothingness
rising out of the bleak northeastern area. At least now there
is a library and library service. It is modest, it has not
yet "sold" itself to the people. But for those who have discovered it, seen its Indian-related books and films, found a
link to the past and to the world outside that they might never have expected--for these people, it must be something of
an oasis. And unlike some other Federally funded services
that have come and gone like mirages, the library is there,
open some 36 hours a week, reaching out via the book van,
and it will be there as long as a dedicated regional librarian
like Marie Jones can do anything about it.

[At a later tribal meeting, the Winnebagos censured
the party who had reported us to the redneck trooper.]

After we had seen a few more small and proud rural
libraries, we visited another regional librarian, this time in
her home near the Kansas border in southeast Nebraska.

The home happens to be that 320-acre cattle ranch we
mentioned earlier in this chapter, and it was a perfect setting on which to wind up our interviews, richly symbolic of
the open spaces, the hard work, and the good souls that make
up library life in Cornhusker country.

You wouldn't find nicer folk than the owners of the
Callaway farm if you had the librarian of the Census Bureau
to help you start looking. Evelyn, a professional librarian

Evelyn Callaway, a regional librarian for the Nebraska State Library Commission, on her 320-acre ranch near the Kansas border.

trained in California and with children's work experience in
the East, is now a regional librarian for the State Library
Commission, helping the small libraries in the southeastern
area to train staff, and solve technical problems or any problem that comes along. The library people are thrifty and
self-reliant when they need to be, but not afraid to ask for
help or to help one another.

Her husband, Cal, is a retired Navy pilot, who, when
he decided to take up ranching in his native Nebraska, did it
right and picked up a degree in agriculture. "But don't ask
me how anyone can make a living at it," he laughed.

He hasn't yet broken even at "breeding grass and turning it into beef," as he calls it, but he is clearly not the sort
to despair, any more than is his wife in her own line of work.
The Callaways came to this ranch six years ago and put an
enormous amount of energy into restoring an old farmhouse.
Soon after it was finished, one of Nebraska's famous lightning
storms decended upon them like an artillery shelling. A
block-wide bolt of lightning reduced the house to ashes. Everything was lost--even their beloved and irreplaceable collection of nature and science books. There would be more such
storms; no lightning rod or other device was big enough to
protect them against it.

But they stayed. They built again, converting a trail-
er into a pleasant, permanent cottage, and from the windows
of it they can still watch those block-wide bolts ripping up
the terrain around them and casting an eerie light on the new
book shelves.

But the openness of Middle America holds them. They
have created their own oasis, and they have helped others
sustain theirs.

Another Big Red

The Big Red from the University of Nebraska whipped
their number-one rival a few weeks later and were off to the
Orange Bowl. Football mania was likely to become even
more maniacal. It will be months before Nebraskans can
remember what those other two things were that they are
Number One in. We never did find out ourselves, but we
know that they are not quite Number One in library services.
And yet, by God, you look at those empty spaces and think
that they've actually got libraries out there with new books
and with controversial titles, and you've got to hand it to
them.

Another Big Red, the People's Republic of China, was
admitted to the United Nations the evening we ended our visit
and soared out of Omaha en route to New York. A lot of
Cornhuskers aren't so big on that Commie Big Red; but they'll
be able to learn just about anything related to it through
their local libraries. And they are very big on that.

Chapter Three

(Who speaks for) THE (midwest library) PEOPLE, YES!

Interviews in the Heartland

For about ten days after our romp through the silvery brome
and golden husks of Libraryland, Nebraska, we kicked around
through the broken glass of New York, hands in pockets, head
down, trying to think of how we could express an Easterner's
point of view about Library Life in the Heartlands--a mixture
of deep respect, exhilarating discovery, some distaste, and
some disappointment--without the Easterner's inevitable tone
of paternalism and condescension. We put off our writing up
of the experience for a while, but even later, with emotion
recollected in tranquility, it was difficult to judge the validity
of our most sincere--but very sweeping--views of an entire
aspect of American culture.

    And yet it was already time to set off on the second
leg of our adventure--and adventure seems to be the right
word. For in this series on the library world of Middle
America, we are hunting down the most dangerous species
of all: that which is "typical," "average," "representative."
Of course, one knows at the outset that the greatest trophy
he will come away with will be a feeling about a group of people, something distilled from a thousand observations, re-
sembling at best an a posteriori insight into scientific truth,
and, at worst, a posterior-end-up view of reality--in short,

a biased piece of trash. But if the gamble is great, at least
the stakes are high: for, let's face it, in the national library
press there is very little truth and even less soul concerning
library life in middle America, especially rural M. A. First,
because that life, from what we've seen of it, is a quiet one
relative to the barbaric yawp of the coastal cities, and editors
rarely have time to leave the roar of the highway to listen to
the growing of the grass. Second, because to find the drama,
the meaning, and the moods behind the thousands of library
activities so prosaically, so politely, reported in newsletters
from Middle America, one must go to the Heartland itself,
find the people who have the strongest feelings, and shake
them out. Sometimes it is better for an outsider to do the
shaking to get the outsider's perspective--or bias, if not
careful.

This is what we set out to do: to find the people;
get them to talk; find some meaning through perspective; and
be careful.

We were back from Nebraska. About to begin was
the very first Midwest Library Conference ever--Nov. 3-5,
1971, in Chicago--providing a superb chance for us to talk
with many librarians from Illinois, several from Michigan,
Wisconsin, Indiana, Iowa, Minnesota, Missouri, and Ohio--
and to watch them interact with one another.

And so, as November crept into the Bronx on little
rat paws, we high-tailed it from the Borough of the Broken
Bottles to the City of the Big Shoulders.

Prologue

"Okay," we said to ourselves, our feet planted firmly
on the drafty floor of Chicago's Sherman House. "This is

the Midwest Library Conference; we are standing in one of
the registration lines; ergo, we are surrounded by Midwest
librarians."

We looked around. Already gathered were hundreds
of the 2,200 persons who would register within the three days
of the conference. There was a gentleman in a turban with
very dark, exotically twirled whiskers. There were lanky,
long-haired women with a liberated look in their eyes such
as we had just left in Fun City. There were men, too, in
what we thought to be the New York mold--bushy locks,
moustache running into the sideburns, tinted, oversize lenses,
attire boldly flared at the extremities; in the hubbub there
were Southern accents, Newark accents, black inflections,
Jewish inflections, even Bronx accents! Momentarily, we
panicked. Blast this melting pot of a tribal American culture! What kind of story was this going to be?

(CHICAGO, NOV. 3--A reporter making a special trip here
from New York to investigate, as he phrased it, the differences between library life in Middle America and in the
coastal, urban areas, discovered, within ten minutes, that
people were the same everywhere. He spent the rest of his
visit at the Shedd Aquarium.)

But suddenly--ah--we spotted two of the cleanest-cut
young ladies one could imagine; conservatively, but perfectly
attired and groomed in every detail; beige suit; plaid suit;
white blouses. In their voices was the flat "A" (C-A-T
equals kee-at) of no native New Yorker, and in their manner
a shyness of no woman who had ever ridden a subway, fought
a Fifth Avenue shopping crowd, or faced the nation across a
big-city reference desk. We approached them. Both had
grown up in the Midwest; both had attended a genteel library

school in the Midwest (which we later visited); both worked
in genteel Midwest suburban libraries outside Chicago--in
white, white-collar communities; both said that there would
have to be a pretty good reason for them ever to leave the
Midwest.

They were Midwestern to the core! And so, seeking
reassurance that we would, indeed, find profound differences
in library life East and Midwest, we asked: "What are some
of the biggest problems in your libraries?"

"Theft," they said.

They could have knocked us over with a bookmark.
Theft! We thought we'd just _left_ Rip-Off territory. And
just ten days earlier, based on our Nebraska experience, we
had believed that honesty was one of the things you could
usually count on in Middle America.

But it wasn't twenty-four hours later that we were
reading in the Chicago Tribune the headline: STATISTICS
SHOW CRIME IS BIG BUSINESS IN THE SUBURBS.

Their other problems, too, had a familiar ring. Lack
of space; too much work and not enough appreciation by the
public; small members of library systems bucking the system
headquarters--particularly on book selections that the local
librarians considered offensive.

_No_ way! we thought. "No _way_ to find the typical Midwesterner and distinctive Midwestern library problems by
going after external, superficial signs and symbols.

Instead, we would go to the First General Session of
this Midwest Library Conference, and we would listen to a
discussion that promised to be revelatory of human nature in
general: a group of people were going to try to agree on
something. In this instance, on federating all their various
State library associations. Later, we would talk to the people
individually.

The Prelims

If, some years from now, the Midwest Federation of
Library Associations becomes so established it takes on an
acronym that is MFLA'd about in every library circle, don't
let any myth-maker tell you it was born either momentously
or majestically, as some believe about the birth of ALA.
Out of committees, prior to this session, had oozed a "Temporary Bylaws" for the new federation. The two or three
hundred "rank-and-file" Midwestern librarians now present
were to give "feedback" on the idea, and the feedback would
provide "input" to the State associations which had not already
supported the idea (Indiana, Iowa, and Ohio had). Are you
asleep yet? You can see that it wasn't exactly the sort of
birth at which rockets flare or angels sing. In fact, the
group was so sluggish at the first call for action, it looked
like the poor MFLA baby would have to be dragged out by
the heels.

But it picked up.

The people were reacting to a federation which, ideally, would promote cooperation and avoid duplication among the
member associations. There would be a Midwest regional
conference every four years. Each State association would
elect one executive board member; each would be taxed on a
per capita basis.

The audience quickly divided into two camps. One was
the Common Sensicals: anything that promotes cooperation,
avoids duplication, makes for bigger and better conferences has
got to be okay. The second was the Suspicious Citizenry: anything that sets up a hierarchy, removes decisions another step
away from the rank-and-file members--creates another executive board ruling the masses from behind closed doors--is very
highly suspect, indeed.

In between these warring camps was a civilian who
was beginning to wonder how she ever wandered on to this
battlefield: Mary Ann Swanson, supervisor of media services,
Evanston Town (Ill.) High School. Though she was only an
agent of an idea developed by many others, she quickly became a scapegoat for those who thought it was one idea whose
time had not yet come. The arguments were often directed
at her personally, with wagging finger. We don't think a
New Yorker would have shown such "grace and aplomb," as
the Wisconsin Library Bulletin described it later. We think
she might have thrown a water pitcher or two at someone.

But did the people say "yes" to the idea? By and
large, it seemed that, yes, they would be taking positive
recommendations back to their State associations. Will the
State groups say "yes?" Robert McClarren, who organized
the conference, thought so. And so did we. It was a feeling
we got that they fight, these Midwesterners, but eventually
they say yes to an idea not totally outrageous. Does it matter to anyone outside the Midwest if the group federates? By
one measure it could. As Eileen Cooke of the ALA Washington Office pointed out in a later general session, the eight
States in the group are represented by about one-fourth of the
total U.S. Congress. [4]

We attended a few other large sessions, but the Midwestern voice was being drowned out by the universal jargon
and clichés of library meetings. Now it was time, without
further delay, to sit down with some individuals who looked
like they were bursting with pent-up points of view, and to
let it all gush out onto our notepad. We didn't tape inter-
views--people wax rather phony and turgid into a microphone.
But we talked. We relaxed with some over coffees, cornered
others on the run. But always, with a squeeze of the arm,

Heartland interviews: "Behind a cloud of pipesmoke Emil
Levenson ... mused about his years as a Midwest librarian."

a tilt of the head, a lilt of the voice, we indicated--we plead-
ed--that they level with us. We think they tried.

But so much for the scholarly methodology. Now, on
to:

The Heart (Land) of the Matter!

We were sitting at a table in a small hospitality area.
Behind a cloud of pipesmoke Emil Levenson twirled his moustache and said Eastern things like "zeitgeist" and "vibrancy"
and he mused about his years as a Midwest librarian. We
knew he was digging for substance, as was Georgia Voelker,
also at our table, delivering her thoughts to us in great rich-
earth-shoveling motions of the hands.

Emil was a public librarian in Newark, New Jersey,

Georgia Voelker, who grew up in Iowa, delivered her thoughts
to us in great rich-earth-shoveling motions of the hands.

ten years ago. A former library school lecturer in Madison,
Wisc., now he is a Ph.D. candidate there and assistant librarian of Oak Park, Ill. He was comparing East and Midwest.

"Yes," he said, "there is a vibrancy here ... it's
good ... but the pace is slower. In Newark there was a
sense of problem. Trust? mmm ... It's been easier to build
trust in a suburban community like Oak Park."

"But you know," said Georgia, who grew up in Iowa
and now runs the outreach program for the Madison Public
Library, "the unserved groups here are not as obvious. The
problem doesn't seem as pressing because it's harder to identify. Madison is mostly a professional town. The same poverty people are being surveyed by everyone because there are
so few of them.

"The entire Mexican-American and black population is
only about two percent. A lot of East Coast programs can
just take a bookmobile and sit there and wait. We have to
go out and make personal contact.

"There's no more trust here than anywhere. We have
to build it by not making promises unless we can deliver.
We don't build it by taking sides among the various mixed,
hostile groups in town, even though it's hard not to. But
things still don't always work out. Our program in South
Madison was a bust as far as the local blacks were concerned.
For one thing, we didn't have a black librarian working it."

"That's a problem here," Emil said. "Most black librarians seem to be committed to programs in the East and
Southeast."

"... We don't connect outreach with any one category
of patron such as low-income, minorities, etc.," Georgia
said a little later. (It seemed to us a good point to remember

in our search for the Midwest differential.) "People here
have tremendous community pride. But sometimes it makes
them ostrich-like; they don't want the kind of library publicity
that points out community problems. They don't even see the
problems they don't want to believe. So our outreach program
is directed at all levels of taxpayers who for some reason
have been unserved. "

Emil picked up the theme. "In Northwestern Wisconsin, the Indians and rural dairy farmers--who are getting
practically no library service--have a low average income,
but they don't think of themselves as 'disadvantaged.' They
feel they're in a temporary, monetary bind. You must consider how your clients define themselves. "

Emil was lecturing, digressing a little from what was
peculiarly Midwestern, but you couldn't fault him for it: he
had lectured at Madison on "The Library in Society," which
was one heck of a course, according to his former student,
Miss Voelker.

We asked about the Midwesterner's sense of place--
the feelings about outsiders. Georgia replied that, yes, there
is that sense, people do identify closely with their home territory, and that it is very difficult for a new librarian to become an insider. She will often be brushed off with: "Well,
you're not from here. " The problem of being an outsider
compounds the more general problem of community involvement by librarians: how does one get involved, get one's
hands dirty in local struggles, and maintain that good old professional aloofness and impartiality? The answer, according
to Georgia:

"Librarians in the Midwest are not really involved in
municipal politics. "

"For any kind of political involvement, " Emil added,

"you'd better have your board behind you. The librarian at
Oshkosh did, for instance, after he raised his flag halfmast
during a war moratorium. The community was up in arms,
but he was able to stand his ground."

Both Emil and Georgia offered the analysis, without
prejudice, that Midwesterners seem not to concern themselves
overly with abstractions, but to deal with the concrete. You
talk concrete details first with Midwest librarians and clientele, then you philosophize and generalize. The agrarian
world view vs. the urban--and all that. Emil felt that the
abstract approach lent dynamism to library movements arising in the East, and he was disappointed to hear from us that
some of those Eastern reform groups had become about as
dynamic as mudpie; that despair and frustration seemed to
be undermining commitment on several fronts. We set him
off.

"A librarian _must_ realize a personal, existential commitment to library service! Funds don't mean a thing for
libraries. Just get some librarians who give a damn! Who
care about _people_."

And could such librarians find happiness in the Midwest, in Middle America?

The fact that neither Emil nor Georgia have any in-
tention of leaving provided us with one answer. Emil put it
another way:

"It may not be where it's happening--but it's where it
can happen. It's up to you."

The Ghosts of Easterners Past

Even though all Midwestern librarians do not come
from the East--honest!--the next four who stopped by our

table were, indeed, shadowed by the ghosts of their Eastern pasts. Not only that, but they were all public librarians, and all had something good to add about working in the Midwest. You'd have thought we'd put out a New York strawberry cheesecake to attract them, but more likely they were drawn in by Georgia's reaping gestures.

One ghost of Elliott Kanner's past was the poverty of New York's Lower East Side, where he began his life. Now he is resources coordinator for a library system (North Suburban System, Ill.) with a generous State grant on a per capita basis--and with thirty-three percent more of those capitas in 1970 than the previous year! Although Elliott doesn't always like the reasons for the suburban migration, he likes the kind of unheard-of-in-the-East support that Illinois gives to all its library systems. In short, he likes having some resources to coordinate. Wouldn't you?

Sydelle Popinsky of Newburgh, N.Y., a shabby ghost town, Hudson-Valley style, hasn't exactly escaped to Xanadu; she's a reference librarian now in Rockford, Ill., a big, conservative, Middle American industrial city. She had only been there eight weeks, dishing out cultural information in art, music, and literature, and trying to motivate some of the high school kids who come to the library under very "external" motivation. Can an Eastern dispenser of "culture" find happiness in the industrial heartland?

So far she's having a ball. The library collection is good, her own cultural life fulfilling.

"In the Midwest, you may have to work at achieving a global perspective, but it's possible. You can keep in touch with things, get away from the parochial, when you want to."

Another with Eastern experience who simply "wouldn't

go back" is Tom Forte, a neat, fashionably attired young
Chicago Public Library administrator who has probably put
more library books and services directly into the hands of
the previously unserved than any single librarian in the nation.
If you haven't heard of him--well, that tells you something
about his commitment to his work and his community.   The
sense of community in a large Eastern city is, at best, no
greater than that occasionally found at the neighborhood level.
But, according to Tom, "You can feel that you belong to Chicago.   There's more togetherness here."   Tom believes that
the togetherness can cross racial lines as well--a tricky business in a city that has been rated as the most segregated in
the entire nation. 5   In his own experience, however, there
has never been one militant encounter regarding the four
black service centers set up by the library.

Does belonging to Chicago mean belonging to Mayor
Daley?   Another informant told us that it isn't so bad for
the library, which, politically, is in pretty good shape.   "Oh,
of course," she said, "when Boss came out, a precinct com-
mitteeman called up and said don't push the book.   But we
could certainly carry it."

Our fourth Eastern-reared Midwesterner, a former
New Yorker now working as a librarian in Chicago, had recently been a free-floating librarian in Gary, Ind., a town
where men drink a shot of whiskey--glass and all--in their
beer.   In order to remain relatively free and floating, she
asked not to be named.   But she went ahead and said nice
things about the Midwest anyway:

"I was," she confessed, "an Eastern chauvinist in the
Heartlands for a long time.   But finally I've come to prefer
it here.   Even in Chicago, the people are more open, less
cynical.   There's more hope here--maybe because there's

more space. You can escape the oppression of a city very
quickly. But Chicago is a city that works, as they say.
There's a strength to it. "

Prairies and Corn

Midwesterners, we learned quickly get tired of Eastern clichés about the wide open spaces, and you can't even
rely on the theory that more space yields more hope. For
one of the less hopeful library outlooks we encountered had
to do with some sections of wide open rural Illinois.

Among the State's eighteen library systems are some
with names that are journalists' dreams: Starved Rock, Lincoln Trail, Cumberland Trail, Lewis & Clark, Rolling Prairie,
and Corn Belt. We were lucky enough to nab representatives
of the last two for a little chat and comparison of notes
about rural library life.

Diann Peabody of Rolling Prairie is a country-beauti-
ful young woman who, though a little reticent about talking to
a reporter, nevertheless spoke with apparent feeling and sin-
cerity about her system. She knows something about the
rural world: she grew up in a town of 500, and her libraries
serve many towns not much larger. Or at least they are located in the towns. As to how many of the townsfolk they
serve and how well--Diann was worried. She believes strongly in the systems concept, is against the proliferation of what
amounts to isolated local reading rooms; but not all libraries
in her area agree with her. Sometimes their opposition
seems more irrational than independent: "Some libraries
thought the State was going to take away all their books and
give them to other libraries. " The system libraries try to
reach out to the farm families with bookmobiles and special

materials, but too often "the farmer's family members are
users, not the farmer himself.   All he uses are three jour-
nals, <u>Prairie Farmer</u>, <u>Successful Farming</u>, and <u>Farm Jour-
nal</u>." Another factor preventing the "reading rooms" from
becoming active and aggressive libraries is the number of
professional librarians that can be hired for these small Central Illinois communities.   Out of the twenty-eight library
"directors," only three have library degrees.

Henry Meisels is no less concerned about the effective-
ness of his twenty-one-library Corn Belt System.   But even
as he shared his worries with us, he projected more plucki-
ness than pessimism.   Perhaps it had something to do with
his shining, avuncular features, the crow's feet around his
eyes--but at least there were none of the grimaces and throw-
ing down of the hands you often run into when a New York
librarian tells his problems.

"I'm afraid," he said, referring to his Corn Belt System, "that the library is not really essential in the minds of
those who must pay the money for it.   There is no real understanding of its purpose and whether it's worth the taxes.   The
libraries are bypassed by the Now Generation.   Why?   It's a
combination of circumstances.   The buildings are worse than
the old Carnegies.   In this age of cars, we can't even get
parking lots--the only buildings without them in these communities.   And who's going to tell the story of what a library
environment means to a young person?   The young people
who don't inherit the father's farm go off to the cities and
become the disadvantaged.   But they don't come back to warn
the others."

And even if they did bring the message: "Start en-
riching your lives before it's too late," would the libraries,
as they are now, be able to help them?   Henry wasn't sure.

"The way it's run now, the staff members are limited
in what they can select. How they can build their local collections. And the staff itself--many of the trustees are reluctant to replace some of the ancient institutionalized, local
librarians. "

We nodded sympathetically, making a long face. Henry grinned. "Listen, there's plenty of good in this system. "
And, perhaps thinking of the per-capita circulation figure for
it, which, like Rolling Prairies, is a very solid eight, he
added, "It's not all so bad. "

There was a brief pause in our conversation with
Henry and Diann, when suddenly, like a windstorm blowing
from the west across the Mississippi and into these calmer
plains, there came into our midst a robust and beaming
Nellie Neafie, head of the Seven River Library System, Iowa
City, Iowa. Couldn't help overhearing our talk about rural
service--had a few ideas on that herself.

"When a farmer asks me for some information, I get
it for him if I have to pick it out with my teeth! One farmer
made $3, 000 with the information I got him, and now I've
got that county sewed up for the library. But I've got thir-
teen more counties to worry about. Now Iowa's TWX--that's
what makes a small library a big library. But we cannot
ignore, we cannot abort, we cannot assimilate the little libraries. Who wants to be a branch?" Nellie stopped just a
split second to catch her breath. "Now I'll tell you about a
one-thousand-person town that voted two-to-one for a $10, 000
library expenditure. "

She described how the town remodeled the fire house
into a library, and how much this kind of local expenditure
meant relative to the limited funds available from the State.

"Come out and see us!" she urged. "Bring money!

"... suddenly, like a windstorm blowing from the west across
the Mississippi and into these calmer plains, there came into
our midst a robust and beaming Nellie Neafie, head of the
Seven River Library System, Iowa City."

Sorry I interrupted. G'bye!"

She was off like the wind again, but what she'd said
stuck with us. And it was interesting that her money worries were something we didn't often hear from the Illinois librarians. That funds are not their most haunting problem in
these lean times has to do very much with one extraordinary
and controversial man.

A. F. Trezza: The Music He Hears

In a recent article on his Illinois State Library, [6] Director Alphonse F. Trezza closed with the Thoreau lines
about a "different drummer. Let him step to the music
which he hears, however measured or however far away."
The words are favorites of Al's, and whatever else might be
heard about this most powerful librarian in Middle America,
you will never hear that he steps to anyone's music, any beat,
but what he personally believes is the true, the just, and the
beautiful.

And what is the music he hears? When you talk with
him, as we did at the Midwest Library Conference, you have
the feeling that there are seventeen symphonies, six ragtime
bands, and a few drum and bugle corps all going at the same
time--and all in perfect harmony. Never make the mistake
of asking him a question for which you do not want the complete answer, all implications and ramifications, a related
discourse on library administration, and a theory of library
service.

Because he is always ready with particulars as well
as general theories, and because he can express them with
the speed and precision of a tommygun, he has been unusual-
ly successful at getting money for his libraries. He believes

that libraries should get plenty of support from the State, and Illinois' unique State Library setup had enabled him to make it a supportive one thus far: the Illinois Secretary of State also bears the title State Librarian, and the Director of the State Library reports directly to him. Thus, for the library, there is a direct link into the inner politics of the State; but two factors must be present before it does anyone much good: you must have a State Library Director who can talk you to Timbuktu and back about libraries--i. e. , Al Trezza--and you must have a State Librarian who will listen. Since Al took office in 1969 (after eleven years of high executive staff office in the American Library Association, Chicago, Ill.), he has had two good listeners: Paul Powell, who, for all his shoe-boxes full of dough, left enough to get the public library sys-tems going full blast, and his successor, John W. Lewis, who has helped keep them going--along with Trezza, State Library staff members, and some LSCA-I federal money.

The music Al Trezza hears includes the martial beat of tight organization, structure, law and order, rhyme and reason--and action. In his article (op. cit.) he wrote: "The emphasis on a strong State Library having legal authority and financial support and the need for a coordinated statewide li-brary system has been the underlying theme which the direc-tor ... and his staff have tried to implement in the past six-teen months.... Continuing efforts to assert responsible leadership by action rather than talk is essential.... Activ-ism after all is the order of the day not only for militant students and radicals but for those in librarianship who be-lieve that major efforts in a new direction for a truly co-operative program are basic...."

While he stresses that cooperative programs must be arrived at through democratic dialogue, he implies that there

Al Trezza against a background of himself. He steps "to the music which he hears," which has made him the most forceful librarian in Middle America.

is little patience with those who lag behind or obstruct the
will of the majority.

As a result partly of Al Trezza's beliefs and methods,
some 477 out of 505 tax-supported public libraries, representing 98 percent of the population and 97 percent of the
geographic area, were encompassed by the network of systems as of last spring. [7]

His influence is not limited to statewide librarianship.

Almost as a direct result of Al Trezza's beliefs and
methods, the American Library Association was able, at its
Midwinter 1972 Meeting, to activate the Office for Minority
Recruitment when there had appeared to be no funds immediately available for this membership and Council mandate.

By using federal funds to set up a State pilot recruitment
project that would, in effect, serve national purposes as well,
and by arranging to have the American Library Association
administer the project, Al pulled it off.

Finally, as a direct result of Al Trezza's beliefs and
methods, there are some who consider him a dictator, a little Napoleon, a staunch member of the "establishment," and
all his talk just a lot of hot air.   But unless there is reference to his humanitarian motives, which he will very strongly
defend, he is not overtly offended by those who fight against
him.   Nor by Illinois librarians who fight one another.

"We fight, but we fight together," he told us.   "None
of this 'we'll take our marbles and go home.'"   He described
a rift between Illinois school librarians and the other librarians, and how he appealed for cohesion in order to achieve
legislative success.   As for system members who balk at
reciprocal borrowing, he urges them not to forget they're in
today's world--the ability to give the customer total library
service should come before everything else.

Because Al is an Easterner who came to the Midwest
eleven years ago from Philadelphia, we asked him to talk
about the two societies for a moment. This slowed him down
a bit; he probably hadn't stopped to think about it for the past
decade. "Well," he said, "I guess maybe there's more culture in the East. But Midwesterners aren't any more re-
sistant to change than anyone else. Hell--people are the
same everywhere.

What About Those School Libraries?

Out of the thousands of school librarians in Middle
America, we were able to talk at any length only to one from
Oak Park, Ill., and another from Milwaukee, Wisc., at this
conference. Still, we can come up with one mighty generalization, if you'd like: they got rich school libraries and
poor ones out there.

Selma Richardson runs a rich one. The students of
Oak Park High School still benefit from the Knapp School Libraries Project that ended there about three years ago. Unlike some Knapp libraries, Oak Park has retained the staff
positions developed during the project--and they are still valid,
according to Dr. Richardson, who has an E.D., and knows
her stuff. Hers is a Midwest school from which about 80
percent go on to college; a school that contains a free school
set up by students and now numbering about 150. Located
near the library, the free school develops its own curriculum
and field work. "Some of what they do will infiltrate into
the 'main' school program," Dr. Richardson told us.

Dr. Richardson grew up in Pittsburgh, went to school
in the Midwest. Sister Elaine Basche grew up in Menasha,
Wisc., and has never left a four-State area of the Midwest.

Michigan library trustee Ruby Pratt: "When you think of a Midwesterner, do you envision a black?"

Sister Elaine Basche of Menasha, Wisc., was working with
a $1000 acquisitions budget in her school of 600, but had no
desire to be elsewhere.

For the 600 students at St. Mary's Grade School, there is
only a total of $1,000 budgeted for library resources, and,
although ESEA-II funds have helped in the past, the outlook
for the future is not bright. It doesn't discourage Sister
Basche. She goes on learning how to give better service,
continuing her education through a two-way telephone course
originating at the University of Wisconsin library school.
As a professional librarian in her diocese, she's a rarity,
but in her desire to stay right where she is, whatever the
problems, she is probably not so unusual among Midwestern
school librarians.   That's a feeling we got, and you can call
us down if you know better.

Some of Our Best Friends

We were called down sooner than expected for our rosy
view of commitment to the total community in the Midwest.
Perhaps we'd been talking to too many outreach librarians.
But when we talked to Ruby Pratt, a library trustee in High-
land Park, Mich., a Friend of the Library, and a black woman, she told us what we'd so often heard in the East: "Librarians are not being trained for inner-city work. They run
to the suburbs. They're not trained to serve all the people;
they're afraid of people."

Wayne Kelty, a friend of Ruby's, and chairman of the
Michigan Friends of the Library, underscored her remark
and added, "We want to develop a workshop ... get trustees,
Friends, and librarians together ... set up some inner-city
field work."

Ruby wasn't talking only about service to the blacks.
She specified that senior citizens, too, were among the unserved in her community. But still, we asked her what it

was like to be black in the Midwest. Did she personally have
a feeling of being something called a Midwesterner?

"Am I a Midwesterner?" she smiled. "To me, yes.
To you, no. To you, I'm a black person first. When you
think of a Midwesterner, do you envision a black? But I see
everyone first as humans, anyway. I never felt any black
differentiation when I was a child--I identified with the Snow
Queen. My teachers in Detroit taught black literature and
black heroes right along with the others--yet we could still
have a sense of black consciousness and pride."

Later we talked to another black trustee, The Rev.
Obie Rush of East St. Louis. Like Ruby, the reverend was
as beautiful and pleasant and sincere a person as you could
talk to. But he was one of the last that we chatted with at
the conference, and, frankly, he brought us down so low with
the story we drew out of him, that our great big bubble of
Middle American affirmation almost went down like the Hin-
denburg. He told us how this burg across the river from
St. Louis was an industrial city just making it before the
economic slump, and how jobs had closed up so tight now
that 12,000 had left the city altogether; how the schools were
in such bad shape, the teachers were striking, and how morale was rock bottom--with just one exception: James E.
Williams, a black man, was now mayor, and for the great
black population of East St. Louis there was new hope, a
lessening of the credibility gap between the government and
the people. Finally, he told us that, although there are other black library trustees, there are no black library administrators.

Appointed by Mayor Williams, the young Rev. Rush
had never been a library trustee before, and he was reading
everything related to his new responsibilities. And among

these readings were some on institutional racism.

"I've been reading up on it," he said. We were sitting in the Sherman lobby, watching dozens of Midwest library administrators milling about. "I've been reading up on it, and I look around here...." He released a sigh that seemed to go all the way back to his boyhood in a small Mississippi town and return through the troubles he'd known. "And I look around here ... and I see we aren't anywhere--we haven't got a thing."

We looked around. The faces were white. We were going to mention that at least Clara Jones, black director of the Detroit Public Library, was at the conference. We were going to say several things. But we didn't. For he was looking at our face, too.

Epilogue

Our spirits were not down long. Like everyone else who doesn't have to live day in and day out with the darkest urban despair, we were not obsessed by it, we didn't want to be obsessed by it, we didn't want to obsess anyone else with it. Life goes on, and with it, a search for the affirmative; and that search, leaving unresolved despair in its wake, may indeed be escapist. But it can also be a form of salvation.

We left the shadows of the Sherman House lobby, and it was a blue, crisp, fleecy, brilliant American day, flags flapping almost hysterically in the Chicago winds, yellow leaves exploding with color as the sun shone through them. Yes, we were in a city that "works," and the elevated train, so smooth, so clean, so shiny, taking us out to visit a library school worked just beautifully.

The Rosary College Graduate School of Library Science,

River Forest, Ill., is in a brand new luxurious library building on a campus as leafy and spacious and cared for as a
royal garden. The classes are held in bright, comfortable
rooms, with colors--yellow, orange, rust--that could liven
up a lecture on serials cataloging. Even the current tuition
at this pleasant, coed school is not too depressing: $60 per
credit. In New York, they call that a free education. Sister Lauretta McCusker, dean, runs a pretty good show, and
the faculty we watched and talked with were lively, witty,
dedicated to good teaching.

     And so our spirits were up again. We were visiting,
after all, a real Midwestern library school, most of whose
students were from the Midwest. We talked with one faculty
member originally from California and with experience in
Philadelphia--another who now feels at home in this area,
enjoys the spirit of cooperation he has found in Midwestern
library life.

     All was Midwestern. All was pleasant. But we also
talked to some students, wondering if perhaps we might catch
one faint vibration about the Midwestern librarians of the future. But those few we talked with did a lot of shrugging.
They weren't particularly committed to what they were learning at the library school, nor to their future in the Midwest.
It was late in the day, and unfortunately we were unable to
talk to more students, enough to give us some insurance
against a conclusion that could be overturned by the next
graduating class.

     But we were still willing to generalize that Library
Life in Middle America, in the Midwest, is an affirmative
one--if only because the librarians have an affirmative feeling
about the land in which they work. Many are absolutely and
unshakeably committed to it geographically. Others who wander

off may find themselves rootless elsewhere; even the memory
of one year on the leafy, gentle, Rosary campus could pull
one from some faraway asphalt jungle back in search of the
Middle American dream of a clean well-lighted life.   Where
the people of, say, East St. Louis will find it is a good
question.   But it is not an impossible one.

The "yes" of library life in Middle America is not
only expressed in abstract terms such as solid roots, wide-
open spaces, trust, cooperation, and such other elements as
we identified after our visit to Nebraska.   You will find the
Midwestern library affirmation in thousands of concrete manifestations:

In Chicago's Special Extension Services, working with
dozens of community programs as a resource center, in the
library's active Education Department.

In the Michigan communities that have, with citizen
contributions, raised beautiful new or remodeled library build-
ings--the "library on the lake" at East Grand Rapids; an ugly
duckling of a building transformed into a graceful swan in
Zeeland.   The Windsor Township Library; Gaines Township;
Muskegon County.

In Hennepin County, Minnesota, which enjoyed a 20-
percent circulation increase during 1971.

In the togetherness of CLIC, Minnesota's Cooperating
Libraries in Consortium.

In the half-million-persons benefitting from services
provided by the Mideastern Michigan Library Cooperative.

In the cooperative groupings of both public and school
libraries in Wisconsin.

In the aggressive and affirmative new public library
standards just adopted by the Illinois Library Association.

In such bold programs at the Minneapolis Public Library as bus tours of "alternative cultures" for young adults.

In a new State grant for public library services to six prisons in Illinois, under Louise LeTendre, chief of library services for the Department of Correction.

Just as you will find negation, the "no" of library life in Middle America, manifested:

In the increasing segregation of Chicago's public schools (The New York Times, Nov. 28, 1971, p. 69).

In a Ph.D. study on censorship in the Midwest (Ohio Library Association Bulletin, Oct. 1971) purporting that only 22 percent of the public librarians are strongly opposed to censorship practice, 14 percent are sympathetic toward it, and 64 percent neutral.

In the January announcement from the Cleveland Public Library that 133 hours of service would have to be slashed at ten neighborhood branches as a result of drastic financial problems, problems that could "signal the end to quality library services in Cleveland," according to Director Walter W. Curley.

In The People Yes, Sandburg wrote that there are heroes among the Midwestern people, that they give it all they've got and don't ask questions--and what more do you want? Perhaps in 1936, such a sentiment was considered a form of affirmation. But things change. Chicago is no longer Hog Butcher for the World. And people, in East St. Louis, South Chicago, everywhere, are asking questions. Library heroics in Middle America has come to mean not only giving all--but questioning, again and again, giving all what, to whom, and why.

Chapter Four

The Small-Town American Library:
An Album

The "Middle" America described in Nebraska and Illinois can
be found in small towns almost anywhere in the nation, at
least as far as library life is concerned. "Middle," in this
case, means ongoing American patterns outside the great, urban crises that make headlines. All the libraries in this "album" are in towns of less than 10,000--and there are still a
great many of them in this country. These scenes of small-
town library life are not presented entirely out of sentimen-
tality, although the yearning to go back to the imaginary
"good old days" afflicts us all from time to time. Yet, nothing here was faked. For instance, the librarian below (Mary
Norman) did break her pose to wave to a friend. These are
aspects of library life as it is, and might not always be. We
wanted to capture them for the record.

The Small American Library is ...

Librarian Mary Norman of Avon, Conn., knows every reader
in town.

Hound and hearth: perfectly natural in Pleasant Valley Public Library, upstate New York.

Part of life at the Pleasant Valley Library in the taking in
of the flag.

... national and local pride;

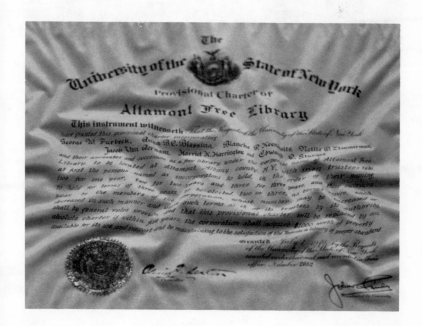

The charter isn't very old yet, but it's history and hung with
pride at the Altamont, N.Y., Public Library.

... A bridge across generations;

Sausalito, California, Public Library.

A game of "Simon Says" at the Litchfield, Conn., Public Library.

... close to God ...

Connecticut.

... and football marching band;

Alabama.

... Young people on their own;

Sausalito, California.

Fairmount Heights, Maryland.

Carnation, Washington.

Avon, Connecticut.

Chapter Five

A Brief Interlude Back "Home" in the Bronx,
Which Is, After All, Mainland America

It was a day like any other at Frank D. Whalen Junior High
School 135 in the Bronx, N.Y., except for those who were
aware that November 19 was also Puerto Rican Discovery
Day.

Two such were the school librarians, Louise Caffin
and Marjorie Ginsberg. They had a program on Rediscovering Puerto Rico all set to go for four classes that day.

Another was Wilson Library Bulletin's associate editor;
we were there with camera for a look at what a fairly average NYC junior high school library is up to these days. Miss
Caffin had sent us some jottings which intrigued us, and, recalling the substantial results from our visit to another "Very
Ordinary American School Library" almost three years ago,
we braved the streets of New York to show up in person.

Actually, JHS 135 isn't in a bad neighborhood of the
wretched Bronx Borough, nor is it the Royal Botanical Gardens. Neither are the kids the cream of Eton; but they aren't
all JDs. They represent a good racial and economic balance,
as the phrase goes, and they range in intelligence from the
little Bobby Fischers all the way down to future bureaucrats
and golf champions. They're wild, but not mean. If it's
still a blackboard jungle, at least no one is shouting "Hey,

101

Teach!" or brandishing switchblades and shooting up during library class. Today we know that the kid who squinted at a reference book and yelled, "Who's Fido Castro?" will grow up to be a great international journalist with such gutsy questions--and with respondents as helpful as were the JHS 135 librarians.

The atmosphere of an American secondary school, as we rediscovered three years ago in the suburbs, hasn't changed as much in the last quarter century as you'd believe from reading educational literature. We're not talking about the carpeted, computerized demonstration schools, but about the JHS 135 variety, where mold-green cinder block walls, Army-green steel shelving, gutter-grey linoleum tiles, and baseball-bat-blonde furniture recall the latest in 1950 school interiors.

When the faculty members gather together, you hear all the traditional arguments about discipline vs. permissiveness, structure vs. free form, closed vs. open classrooms, and so on, but the general feel of the corridors goes back to the closed fifties, with passes required, loudspeakers blaring, disciplinarians--now called deans--rounding up the stray sheep. But who's criticizing? That's too easy. How would we like to run a school in this day and age, when everyone knows all the answers but no one's got the dough? No thanks. We'll stick to what we know--observation--and, to continue, we saw virtually the same cast of characters as appeared in a TV showing the next month of "Up the Down Staircase": concerned teachers, apathetic teachers, and administrators with too much to handle. But does anyone remember the librarian in that film? A prissy and horrible stereotype, she was the one who reminded a teacher that fifteen cents was due on a book from a girl who had just jumped out the window.

Happily, JHS 135 is blessed with something very different in its librarians, although one could fault them in a
few areas if one tried hard enough. But no one's paying us
100 bucks a day to do surveys. So first, let us sing the
praises of unsung heroes. Yes, we know that can get tire-
some as we do it more and more in this book--but someone
has to celebrate the librarians who work in total isolation
from their professional community; who aren't obsessed with
peer approval; who haven't got a prayer of first-class citizenship in their own schools; whose professional relationships
with teaching colleagues and administrators amount to one
long, loud, primal scream about the value of library services,
since so few are listening; and whose one valid motivation
for knocking themselves out is the joy of helping young people
discover, through the microcosmic world of the library,
something about the universe outside.

Are cynics scoffing? They should have seen the fun
these kids and their librarians were having "rediscovering"
Puerto Rico.

Four social studies classes came in for the library
program. (In New York City junior high schools, the librarians teach lessons related to the curriculum. Miss Caffin
prepared a nine-page outline for this day's lesson, in addition
to the special materials she and Mrs. Ginsberg gathered and
put together. So there's one thing the librarians have to do
besides, as they say, "check books in and out.") Each lesson
began with a sound slide show on Puerto Rico with Puerto
Rican music. Some of the kids danced from the waist up in
their seats; others stood and moved in one place to the music.
It was a bit of a downer when the lights came on and the librarian began to talk resources; but the kids stayed with it
and suggested, for a list on the blackboard: the card catalog,

Fresh air makes them a little wild, but the kids of Bronx Junior High School 135 are a good bunch, and the librarian enjoys them.

A Bronx school librarian's main reward is that of librarians everywhere: an occasional show of real interest on the part of library users.

atlases, encyclopedias, Readers' Guide, and so on, as Miss
Caffin effused, "There are so many ways to find things here;
so many materials!" She sent the students after them, and
they came back with little reports to share with the others.
The one who found "Fido Castro" in an index soon discovered
that all Latin surnames are not Puerto Rican--a discovery
every New York anglo has to make at some point in life.
Others found Herman Badillo, former Bronx Borough President and first voting U. S. Congressman of Puerto Rican descent.   The Puerto Rican people in the classes beamed with
pride; there was no doubt that it was their day.

     The pace was insane.   One class was in almost be-
fore the first one was out.   People of junior high age will
get unruly from time to time, and some of the teachers disciplined with something less than respect for fellow human
beings.   One young man asked us, as adults always do, why
we were taking pictures; and before we could tell him, his
teacher snapped, "Would you mind your own business?"
Other teachers left the discipline entirely to the librarians,
who were fairly gentle.   They enforced order only during the
presentations and reports; not during library browsing and
self-discovery of materials.

     The students were serious in their little reports on
resources, if not always on the right track; but it was fun
for us to hear the library research experience expressed now
and then in perfect Bronxese:

     "I went to the cod catalawg and it said the numbah so
I went to it. "

Disparities

     We made no great discoveries during our brief obser-

vations, for we fully expected to find some disparities in the
quality of the various library services.   The school, with
1, 830 students, has a collection of about 10, 000 and a book
budget of $2. 80 per capita; nothing to get excited about.   The
library also maintains a small "Professional and Curriculum
Center" for the teaching staff, but, ironically, the librarians
are not invited to take part in curriculum meetings.   For a
long time the library has had to overcome the impression that
it was just a part of the English Department.

There is talk about AV and modern equipment, but the
library does not even own a microform reader, and the audiovisual materials are still divided up among the departments.
An AV man acquires and maintains the film collection, and,
in talking with him and three or four faculty members, we
were reminded that everyone has a totally different idea of
what a school library should be.

Processing is done centrally, and there are student
library aides to help out with the circulation shtick; but there
is still library work that has to be taken home.

The librarians, Miss Caffin said, enjoy most their
"interpersonal" relationships with the students.   "I don't see
a class, " she remarked.   "I see individual people. "   Still,
not every student name is known by a long shot, and some
students did not yet, in November, know the librarians' names.

From what we could see, however, there was no lack
of love and laughter between librarians and students--something
that all the multimedia materials and a flood of wet carrels
in a bright and carpeted and jazzy IMC cannot guarantee.

Someday, perhaps, there will be both love and luxury
in every school library on the planet.   Work on it.

Chapter Six

Yankee Wool in the Land of Cotton:
A Biased Look at the Libraries of the South

"We're going to leave our Yankee biases right here in New York," we promised.

On the telephone with us was a school librarian in Alabama. We were making arrangements for a journalistic plunge into the Deep South that would take us through Louisiana, Mississippi, Alabama, and Georgia before we surfaced in our Bronx-bound office to gasp for inspiration and understanding, for an approach to the libraries of the South that would reach new depths--for a Northern-based magazine--in fair and accurate reporting.

"Well," said the librarian, "that's just fine...."

There was an unspoken but in the way her sentence tailed off.

"But?" we asked.

"But I don't think you can do it."

Mystique

"... I don't think you can do it."

The words pursued us like a ghost ship at jet speed as we flew to New Orleans; for, ancient mariner that we were in other areas of the library world, we--this writer-- had never before penetrated the Deep South. In our hands

now was one of the works we were reading for spiritual background: The Southern Mystique, by Howard Zinn, who was
raising our hopes by assuring us that the Southern mystique
--that "invisible mist over the entire Deep South, distorting
justice, blurring perspective, and, most of all, indissoluble
by reason"--was now more myth than mystique.

> ... I can say now after living intensely in the Deep
> South in exactly those seven years when the South
> itself has lived most intensely, that the mystique is
> dissolving, for me, and for others. The South is
> still the most terrible place in America. Because
> it is, it is filled with heroes. The South is mon-
> strous and marvelous at the same time. Every
> cliché ever uttered about the South, every stereo-
> type attached to its people, white and Negro, is
> true; a thousand other characteristics, complex and
> subtle, are also true. The South has not lost its
> fascination. But it is no longer mysterious.

Zinn had written those words more than ten years ago,
and we reassured ourselves that, if the clearing trend had
continued, the mist would be so evaporated as to allow us to
see in a week the realities emerging only one by one during
Zinn's seven years.

"Besides," we told the haunting doubts still in pursuit,
"ours is a limited, neatly circumscribed area of concern:
library life." If one understands libraries and their universal objectives, if one understands this constant, then such
variables as are introduced by regional characteristics ought
to be recognized and comprehended as well. Libraries, after
all, are not the major battlefields in a complicated and never-
ending war between the forces of good and evil, right and
wrong. A Yankee or Dixie librarian doesn't fight on one
side, blind to the other. As the mayor of Atlanta himself
put it in 1959, when Zinn was helping to integrate the city's
public library, "A public library is a symbol of literacy,

education, and cultural progress.   It does not attract trouble-
makers. "

Mayor Hartsfield was right; the integration went
smoothly in Atlanta.   As for our own trip?   It, too, went
smoothly.   Southern xenophobia, the suspicion of strangers
which used, they say, to go hand in hand with Southern hospitality, did not show itself in our library visits.   We mingled
with hundreds of Southern librarians at a conference in New
Orleans; we sailed first-class through the libraries of a wa-
tery Louisiana parish; we walked in without warning to warm
receptions in Gulfport, Selma, and Montgomery public libraries, the George C. Wallace Junior College library, and to
the same on very short notice at the University of Southern
Mississippi.   Ours was the only white face visible on the
campus of Alabama State, and we were received, not with
suspicion, but with offers of assistance from every quarter;
we rode a booktruck in the boondocks of Alabama, and no one
shot up our tires; at an integrated high school, as virtually
everywhere else, we took pictures, spoke privately to library
users, threw out questions and comments on whatever came
to mind.   No problems.   In fact, about the only open hos-
tility we ran across was from one Southerner to another, in
defense of the great State of Mississippi, which the second
Southerner had called "last in everything and p-r-r-oud of it. "

So the trip went smoothly.   But the question is, what
did we find?

The answer: everything.

Call it a Yankee bias, call it an outsider's perspective;
but library life in the Deep South showed us "every cliché
ever uttered about the South, " and "a thousand other characteristics, complex and subtle. "

We met librarians who, in perfect innocence, thought

a special collection for blacks meant one of pornography; who told us, matter of factly, "you can always tell a book been borrowed by a Negro; it comes back covered with grease."

We met other librarians, white, who had fought and won their own lonely battle for library integration, equal service, well before the civil rights movement of the Sixties.

We learned of a librarian who is said to have died of strain from rebuilding her library after Hurricane Camille, working night and day in spite of warnings to slow down.

A college freshman recalled her high school librarian in Alabama: "We never went in there. ... He was always mopping the floor and closing the library. You had to wipe your feet. And if you asked him a question, he'd make you feel so dumb...."

We watched another school librarian, white, work as lovingly with her black student aides and clientele as if she'd never known other than the sweet harmony of life together; yet who, in response to a question on her own schooling and if she'd ever shared a schoolroom with a black, cried out, amazed at our ignorance, "Why, Heavens no!"

We saw a richly endowed library doing nothing with everything.

We saw others doing everything with nothing.

We saw a black maid carrying the books to and from a booktruck for the mistress of the pillared old house in which she served.

We saw minority members running minority programs themselves.

In fact, we could have written our story from any angle we pleased, to prove any point, with photographs to back it up. That's often the name of the game in journalism, but it's especially easy in writing about the South, so full of

myths wanting to be upheld or broken down. As in the first
chapter of this book, on West Virginia, we could have written
a story of underdogs struggling against great odds to provide
a decent library service to all peoples; that was generally
true in W. Va. ; but in the South, we could have also told a
story of continuing racism, amateurism, apathy, and services
fifty years behind the times.

We had enough examples to make it a story of honesty
and optimism in library service, as in our Nebraska report;
and we had a few ("Why serve them, " one librarian told us,
"they just don't want what we have. ") with which we could
have drawn a picture of downward- and backward-looking attitudes.

And, echoing the findings of our trip to the Midwest,
we might have slanted a story toward "The New Southern Library Affluence, " knocking down the myth of the po' South;
for there are library buildings--New Orleans Public, Gulfport,
Montgomery, Dadesville, Alex City, Ala. --that come out looking like Holiday Inns and country clubs from the right angle.
But to draw such a picture is not to tell what their operating
budgets are, and what they pay their staff; nor of library
buildings like the Carnegie crypt of Selma, built before the
last black was lynched on a tree nearby.

And the Southern librarians themselves? Who are
they? What do they look like? Again, we could have stacked
the cards in any pattern, from the genteel belles sitting
straight and proper and pure at the New Orleans conference
sessions, to the red-bearded, earringed young man doing outreach with retarded children for the Montgomery Public Library.

And so our trip convinced us that Zinn was right--and
so was the school librarian. The South is but a mirror of

the nation. As different as it often is, there is no mystique,
no mist, to make library life in the Deep South unfathomable
to a Yankee; neither is it possible to view that life without a
Yankee bias. Yet, what is bias but a feeling? Certainly one
can tell what one saw, and then what one felt, thereby avoid-
ing the sweeping generalizations passed off as universal truths,
as the judgment of one group of people by someone who pre-
sumes to know better. None of that here, then. Simply what
we saw, and how we felt. A journal of a trip.

We Bombed in New Orleans

The jet lands softly, cushioned on air as thick as grits,
a humid 80 degrees. The Yankee, entering the Land of Cotton, is wearing wool.

We are beginning our journey in Louisiana, in New
Orleans, where we will have a chance to witness the great
and momentous confluence of two Southern library associations,
hundreds of Southern librarians, coming together here for that
strange and birdlike fluttering about of human beings that wise
men call "conferences." Yes ... the Southeastern Library
Association and the Southwestern Library Association are having a Joint Conference here, beginning this very night, Nov.
1, 1972, continuing for another three days. The two associations have not met jointly for 38 years; they do so about as
often as Haley's Comet crosses Dixie; and so, if we are to
observe the Southern Librarian en masse, we dare not miss
this opportunity.

Here we are then, at the conference. We bomb into
an evening program on "Vibes," an "exploration of the life
style of young adults through music." In an enormous, dark,
and drafty hotel function room, the rock beat quakes, a voice

pontificates and a hundred Southeastern and Southwestern librarians sit straight as pins. We are tuned into "vibes" of our own: in the South, in the South at last, and the function room, the stony conference stoicism on the people's faces, is the same as at any conference. No secrets here ... the evening, for us, a bomb.

And not far away, this same humid night, another bomb: taped to a chair at the Louisiana State University library, rigged to go off when the chair is pulled away from the table.

This we hear on the news as we prepare to invade the French Quarter for the remainder of the evening. For the next four days, Bourbon Street, the street of broken dreams, will belong to the 2,250 librarians and 500 commercial representatives at the conference.

Bombings, broken dreams ... is it symbolism or humidity which weighs so heavily in the air this night?

Jung and the Walls of Jericho

The day is bright and hot. The exhibits, the representatives' displays of library wares, two floors of them, open early and within minutes are flooded with librarians; they are come to market from the outposts of Southern Libraryland, for the displays and merchandise here are slick and first-rate and abundant. The representatives are the big boys of library commerce, not the small fry sent to conferences in the smoky, sullen cities of Middle America. No, New Orleans is a plum--and see all the familiar Northern librarians somehow managing to junket at this Southern gathering! Some were smart enough to dress Southern, even in white shoes, but they are pronouncing the name of this hotel

--the Jung (which Southerners drawl with a softly confessed
"J")--tight-lipped, with hyperborean gloom, as if it were the
name of the psychiatrist, and thus giving themselves away.

Later, we are going to limit ourselves to Library Life
of the Deep South, represented mainly by States within the
Southeastern library group. But we are curious about the
Southwesterners, too, and we drift into their membership
meeting.

They are an enthusiastic bunch, true to themselves.
Some wear western boots. Little corny cracks, whoops, and
hollers from the podium keep the folks chuckling and the production as musical and as knee-slapping natural as it looks
in Oklahoma:

"... and a young lady'll give a kiss to each scholar-
ship fund donor!"

"Whoo-hooo!"

"... and the champagne'll be on me!"

"Whoo-hooo!"

There are all types in the room, of course, but many
of the librarians are women, and many of these as apple-
cheeked beautiful and wide-eyed as the Queens of the Great
American Halftime, perfect posture, never a slump in their
lives; we wonder if somehow they will grow up into those
powerful library women kicking up the Southwestern dust in
their gritty determination and rock-solid abilities to get things
done: the Allie Beth Martins and the Lillian Bradshaws, whose
presence in the room is felt like shadows of Mt. Rushmore.

They are a proud group, these Southwestern librarians.
We hear them talking about something called SLICE, their
mouths watering as if it is a cool melon on their tongues
rather than the acronym for the Southwestern Library Interstate Cooperative Endeavor, a working together of which they

are especially proud; they are also proud of having earned a
national grant that helped turn their association from "mori-
bund" to mission-oriented; and no one who has seen the innovative and progressive library programs rolling out from
the Southwest as briskly as tumbleweed will begrudge them
their new confidence.

We tumble out of the Southwestern end of conference
activities at this point, and, finding little more to our im-
mediate interest in the Jung Hotel than a lone cockroach, we
decide to visit our first bona fide Southern library, the New
Orleans Public, just down the street.

In a town that loves its old buildings and monuments
--even one at the foot of Canal Street which celebrates "white
supremacy"--we expect to find a great gray grotesquerie of
the Carnegie era housing the city's central library collection.
Instead, our preconceptions are pleasantly slapped down by
an airy, bright, and inviting building put up in 1959 but in
tune with modern architecture. Outside, the shiny magnolia
leaves lend a Southern touch, and inside it is clear at once
that here is a library serving every type of Southern minority
as well as the whiteanglosaxonmiddleclassredneckprotestants
we know and serve so guiltily in all regions. It is lunch
time, the place is humming, patrons of every age and class
and color are racing about as if after butterflies or pinning
down a furtive thought at the reading tables. There is an
open, relaxed atmosphere; materials of every kind are available, accessible, up front. The head of technical services
shows us about ... in the New Orleans history room a young
black man in gym shorts and white sneakers jumps from card
catalog to carrel--such enthusiasm! Even the staff library,
its library literature dog-eared, impresses us. Finally, in

Hilda ten Brink, Cuban-born director of New Orleans Public Library's Project Jericho, describes the outreach program for the area's Spanish-speaking and others in need.

the main reading room again, an aide asks us if we wouldn't like to meet the head of the library's outreach program, here known as Project Jericho.

We hesitate; it is a sleepy time of afternoon and we are thinking, when you've seen one urban outreach you've seen them all. But then: "This is the head of Project Jericho," says the aide, pointing to one of the most beautiful and intelligent-looking human beings we have ever seen in our many library travels. "Mrs. ten Brink." We pause, already refreshed.

Hilda ten Brink is Cuban-born, and her Jericho Project (co-administered by the St. Bernard Parish Library) reaches out toward another 15,000 Cubans, 25,000 Hondurans, and some 50,000 others from Latin American countries, as

well as providing special services and/or materials for blacks,
the very young in daycare, and the very old. Outreach in
such a heterogeneous city as New Orleans means turning
away from certain traditional approaches--such as bookmobiles, which didn't work--and building up a people-oriented
service at key library centers, where the service and collections can be many-faceted. The action varies from the provision of bestsellers in Spanish (most popular title: <u>Todo lo</u>
<u>que usted siempre quiso saber sobre el sexo</u>) to teaching
what a library is and does in the first place. One Honduran,
for instance, was upset that there was a wait on a particular reserve title; he wanted to ship it home to his family
right away!

    We are reluctant to leave Mrs. ten Brink and this
pleasant library; only the most important meeting of the conference induces us to return to the Jung--for a special program on the Neighborhood Information Centers Project.

    Surely the hottest topic in public library life these
days is community information: crisis information--survival
information for those citizens shunted about and deprived by
a system grown too complicated, overcrowded, and hostile to
make known what services it does provide. The library has
long seemed to many the logical institution within which to
provide a centralized, coordinated source of such information,
and now a $324,000 Office of Education grant has enabled li-
braries in five cities to set up model projects.

    This afternoon's presentation represents the first for
a group of Southern librarians, and they are interested.
Some 400 pack the small room to hear how each site--Atlan-
ta, Cleveland, Detroit, Houston, and Queens Borough--will
have at least two information centers operating by the beginning of 1973. [8]

Focusing our attention on what will be happening in
Atlanta, the South's entry in this project, we are impressed
as we have been before by Carlton C. Rochell, director of
that city's progressive library, a masterful library politician
whether he is dealing with legislators or committee matrons,
a cool, dark-haired, sleekly dressed man with a mellow Tennessee drawl whose amiability is sometimes answered with
enmity and who can, in fact, be Bogart-tough as he pulls on
his smokes or socks it to you administratively. In Atlanta,
the project is already so popular that every agency and school
wants to get into the act, and the community is calling in for
service before the center is even set up.

Of course, the more southern Southerners say, Atlanta isn't really the South, or at least not the Deep South, so
don't get too carried away by what's going on there. And a
little later we run into John Carter, a Mississipi-reared librarian who has been welcoming the northern Southerners to
"The Real South," and who defines a Yankee as anyone north
of Memphis. He is a likeable fellow who seems to be en-
raging those who ought to be needled a bit, nay, acupunctured,
and we arrange to talk with him at greater length tomorrow.

But first there is an evening, and we pass up a program of staged New Orleans pageantry--a snake dancing mob
led by baton-wielding marshals--in favor of some quieter receptions given by commercial representatives in their hotel
suites. And how suite they are! Rooms with balconies at
both ends, overlooking the gay nightlife of the French Quarter
or into a New Orleans courtyard with palm trees and fish
ponds and candlelit tables. At the Southern Library Bindery
suite, where the Mississippi librarians gather off-hours, we
hear a male Dixie voice crooning to a pretty blonde woman on
the terrace: "Now don't get me wrong, honey. Ruzicka binds
a good book."

Southern maverick librarian John Carter: "You can get away with almost anything in the South as long as you do it politely --and wear a tie."

There is something surreal about standing between
palms and stars in a sweet Southern breeze and hearing such
whispered particulars of the library business.

And in another suite, a representative whose real name
is almost identical to that of the hero in Gone With the Wind
stands as tall and dashingly tailored as Clark Gable and charms
the Scarlett O'Hara's of the library world, who, blushingly
beautiful, listen to library talk with a dreaminess in their
eyes which distinctly says, "I'll think about that tomorrow."

Tomorrow arrives. We are feeling as well as thinking deeply about the South and its librarians because we are
riding with one of them through the bayous of the Mississippi
Delta--we are driving toward Barataria, La., past forests
and along waterways whose foliage is so thick with ghostly
gray Spanish moss that the entire landscape seemed haunted.

We are with a young man named John Carter, raised
about 200 miles up the Mississippi and slightly east, in Jackson. His accent is as smooth as Southern Comfort, his dis-
position like the mellow Dixie sun pouring through the windshield, lighting up his whiskers. Born of a solid local family, he worked in the Jackson Public Library as early as age
18, while a student. After earning his library degree at
Emory, he served at Eastern Illinois a few years, "but Mississippi kept calling me home." Driven by "a kind of Willie
Morris love-hate relationship" with that State, he returned.
There he became, in turn, an academic librarian; a boy wonder of public librarianship; a good Mississippi boy who was
being "led astray"; an academic librarian; and a South Caro-
linian.

The particulars are lengthy. But what emerges from
them as we interview him during the drive is a love of being

Southern and a loathing for (what he considers) the negative
implications of that identification, motivating him to seek a
change in the conditions that give rise to them, and to cleanse
oneself and one's beloved Southern brothers thereby. There
are a great many Southerners, of course, with these same
sentiments, for without them no externally imposed "reforms"
could ever take effect. In Carter's instance, he was given,
at age 27, the directorship of the largest municipal library
in the State--Jackson's--at a time (Summer '65) when outside
pressure was on to integrate the "separate-but-equal" library
system; when SNCC workers would send a group of blacks
alone into the library to test the water, so to speak, while
outside there patrolled the nation's largest per-capita police
force; when the blacks were relegated to the Carver Municipal
Library and when the library board chairman was ready to
close the main library before he'd admit blacks to it or certainly before he'd give them seats.

"Integration is here," the young director decreed to
his staff when he found they were denying services to blacks.
There were more subtle problems, too; the white director of
the local NAACP had been unable to secure a library card in
six months of trying. Carter delivered it to him personally.

"Everyone had told me, 'don't touch this job,' and
they had good reason. But now there was very little trouble
--to my face. It went on behind my back. Still, I was
from a good family, and a native can get away with a lot
more than an outsider; he'll be forgiven for being led astray.
But time went on and I just wouldn't come around and start
to fit into their stereotyped mold of what a library director
should be. The South has these molds, you see...."

Nor did he always fit into it as an academic librarian
of high office in Mississippi, when he took part in a legal

battle for teaching evolution in the schools and acquiring books
about evolution. And so today John Carter is an academic
librarian in South Carolina, a State which is "the subtle
rapier to Mississippi's rusty axe. Mississippi talks about
'integrationists' and 'mongrelization' and 'niggers,' while
South Carolina gently discusses the influence of Communism
on Washington. They both mean the same thing, and they
both know they mean the same thing; the difference is in
style. "9

We drive deeper into the bayou, the Bayou Segnette,
Cajun country, past a pinkish hut of a public library, part
of a system that we are scheduled to explore later in the
week. The conversation turns to Southern library life in general. Is there a difference in the tone of the service--is it
more personal? No, Carter says; he believes that the warm-
er, more personal service of the rural libraries as opposed
to the urban systems would be a better generalization than to
distinguish between North and South.

And what about censorship, intellectual freedom?

The subject is dear to Carter; he has fought the fight,
has spoken of it at length and will speak of it again many
times. The words flow easily:

"Southern censors largely ignore libraries. The South
has always had bigger fish to fry. Who could be bothered
about what was being read when so much was being done? In
the Sixties, who could be bothered with books when half the
population was in open rebellion against the other half and
being murdered for its troubles; when there were riots at
Ole Miss and bombings in Hattiesburg and massacre at Or-
angeburg and Selma.... ?

"As for the freedom of the individual librarian, well
... you can get away with almost anything in the South as

long as you do it politely--and wear a tie. I once tested
this theory by going to work three days straight without wearing one. All hell broke loose! I was called on the carpet
and accused of everything from drinking beer with students
to canoeing on the sabbath!''

Dr. Jung's Cure

Another Southern sun rises to warm our Yankee wool-
ens. We are back in the Jung, recalling yesterday's drive
to the Delta with a first feeling of being truly on foreign soil,
away from the obscuring universals of library life. But library conference life at the Jung Hotel soon cures us of such
reverie. Even the crystal-clear imagery provided so lovingly
yesterday by John Carter is shattered in part. We encounter
him in a lounge with four very dedicated Mississippi librarians
who are shouting him down and giving us another version of
library life in this supposedly impoverished State. "It's
great! Everything's movin' upwards! New buildin's everywhere! Y'all stop off at Pascagoula and see! New pay scale
for public libraries! County networks! Library schools!''

"Four of them," Carter offers, "all unaccredited."[10]

"Now look," says one of the librarians to him, waving
a big-knuckled ham of a hand, "you been out of this State for
two years."

A silver-haired woman in the group glances at Carter,
turns up her nose. "He's been away a lot longer than that,"
she says quietly.

In the Jung lobby, between sessions, we search for
more librarians who look like they might be able to talk soul-
fully and personally--honestly--about library life in the deep
South. We are especially anxious to find some black people

who can describe the life from a brother's or sister's point
of view, but the blacks we see in the lobby--straightened
hair, matronly suits with shirred white blouses, mother-of-
pearl hornrims--may find offense in our attempts to single
them out, and we hesitate to do so. We are too used to
blacks whose appearance immediately bespeaks black pride
and black consciousness, at least to our limited easternwhite-
journalistic point of view. There is one young man who,
though conservatively dressed, has a hip and natural air about
him; we are about to approach him, but he is speaking quietly, shyly with other conferees, then leaves for lunch with
some friends. We make a note to try to find him later.
We introduce ourselves to a few other librarians, a belle
from 'bama, a Baltimorian transplant to Tallahassee ("Oh,
that's the Deep South down there, all right!"), and some others from towns with such tongue-twisting Faulknerian names
that we make a damn fool of ourselves before we can get
them into our notes: "What? Oosa? Ooga? Cata-who?
Wannee-what?" And we marvel that the transplanted librarians can learn enough Choctaw to make it in the South.

But we are really tiring of the conference atmosphere,
anxious to get on the road, into the field; and as we dutifully
attend the remaining receptions, meetings, and joint sessions,
we find relevance only in a report on the Southeastern States
Cooperative Library Survey, a search for means by which to
meet rising library costs through a regional approach. The
results, the recommendations of the survey, will be out in
1974.[11] But survey director Mary Edna Anders gives this
prognosis: "We librarians are goin' to be dragged kickin'
and screamin' into cooperation." (This she proclaims in
"my Alabama drawl," with which it "takes me twice as long
as anyone to say what I have to.")

Finally, we leave the comfort of the conference hotel, this Jungian couch for work-weary librarians, the old conference milieu in which librarians take time out from their humanitarian mission at home to scream at and harass the Great Unserved who happen to be serving them here as waitresses and desk clerks. We leave this comfort for the uncertainty of the road, but on the way out we chat with an academic librarian who is thinking of moving from the South to take a "bigger" job offered to her up North. "It's a good life here," she sighs. "A pool. A maid. A lot to give up for a supposedly better job."

Comfort ... comfort. Comfort if you make a little dough; comfort if you wear a tie and keep your nose clean. Is that one aspect of library life for librarians in the Deep South?

Luckily, we have decided to make no such generalizations, but we think about it as we leave the Jung for good.

Dixie Heaven via Dewey Drive

We are on the road at last! Now Melvil Dewey Drive in a Jefferson Parish suburb of New Orleans may not be Route 66 across the desert, but it is the road that leads us to the first stop on this leg of our field trip, the Parish library headquarters, and we are glad to be there talking to the Parish library administrator, Maurice D. Walsh, Jr. He will take us to far flung branches and lead us to some curious revelations in the course of this hot and humid Monday.

Walsh is himself something of a revelation and a paradox to us. Another Eastern transplant, he has taken wholeheartedly to the South, and he tells us half-jokingly, on this

Sign frames the Jefferson Parish, La., Library Headquarters.
Director Maurice Walsh had the little access road thus
named.

day before the Presidential elections, that the only trouble
with the South is that there aren't enough registered Republi-
cans.   He is ordinarily a very serious man, a military man
--Reserve colonel going for the star--and he has a hard line
on such concepts as the library as a social-service agency
or such clichés as "libraries to the people."   The library's
business is to provide information resources, and ought to
participate in social service programs only to that extent,
not run them.   Running a community information center such
as those described at the SELA/SWLA conference--not in the
library's area of expertise.   As for outreach, Walsh goes as
far as putting up a branch where there seems to be a demand
for it.   If it is not used--as three black branches reportedly
were not--down they come.   Nor did the Cajuns in Lafitte

Maurice D. Walsh, Jr., Librarian of Jefferson Parish, Louisiana.

respond to French-language materials--so no more. Book-
mobiles--subject to the peculiar local problems of floods,
hurricanes, air-conditioning breakdowns--go to new, not established, schools, including segregated schools. Further,
he does not believe a librarian ought to eat, drink, and sleep
librarianship, or carry on with missionary zeal. Provide
every modern service according to the expressed or obvious
demand of the taxpayers, and you are doing your job.

We take his portrait. His spit-shined shoes gleam at
the camera, while his expression, straining toward a smile,
remains guarded.

All these aspects seem to comprise one quickly observed side of Maurice Walsh, a side well suited to the life
of this particular Deep Southern community--described as
largely middle class, aspiring, office and industrial execs,
skilled workers and their families--who want the resources
coming thick and fast from a no-nonsense library. If Walsh
does a bibliography for publication, it is self-balancing--such
as an utterly unbiased "Choices '72" for the elections--or,
as with a bibliography for understanding the police, it balances
out the radical left tendencies of "revolting" librarians elsewhere. He answers only to the straight and stately gentle-
men of the Parish Council, who support him handsomely--
his is one of the best-supported libraries in the State, in
fact. There is no library board, "and I'm very happy," says
Walsh. "If the head librarian can't run his library alone, he
doesn't belong in that position."

His headquarters shop is a picture of efficiency. We
go through it and smell the newness of the books coming in,
we smell the fluids of the new machines and equipment which
help process and organize these books as they speed their way
to the potential 336,000 clients in the Parish. When you visit

At the Charles A. Wagner Branch, Jefferson Parish, they don't circulate cotton--but just about everything else in the collection.

as many libraries as we do, you can begin to size things up
with just a few sniffs--is it new and vital, or old and stag-
nant? The headquarters smells right. In the AV room we
see some of the 1,425 or so prints of films viewed by
118,000 persons last month. The librarians and staff here
seem subdued, but busy, content to be in the Colonel's crack
regiment. Some, who worked in less modern and comfortable surroundings in an old headquarters across the Mississippi, are especially happy to have made the crossing, and they
have a framed certificate to commemorate it.

The certificate is a Walsh creation, and--along with
the drive he had named after Melvil Dewey--one of the light-
hearted touches that emerge from his other side, the human,
the civilian, the spiritual--what have you--and link him more
to the warm-blooded Southern librarians we have been meeting.
To our surprise--for we have also known of him from some
rather testy letters in the national press--we find him gracious, hospitable, trusting, open, likeable. In his libraries
we begin to see contradictions of his stated philosophies--
bulletin boards suspiciously approaching a community information service. He shrugs these off. But we are most moved
by his compassion for the radical left movements in librarianship, his expressed feeling that, "Basically, all men are of
good will. They're trying to do what they believe is best."

After lunch in a restaurant occupying "the oldest plan-
tation in the Mississippi Valley" we stroll along the grounds
to admire the dozens of oaks whose colossal branches, hung
thick with Spanish moss, shade a broad green lawn. Walsh
stops and admires the perfect and classic Southern landscap-
ing.

"I imagine," he says softly, "that Heaven will be something like this."

We drive along a road parallel to the Mississippi, and, with boyish spontaneity, Walsh honors a whim we express and wheels the car up to the top of the levee, where we crunch merrily over a path made of crushed seashells.

We do not have time to drive to certain Parish branches which would provide uniquely Southern characteristics for our camera--a branch at Grand Isle built on stilts to let the hurricanes pass through, a branch deep in bayou forest country --but at a small, one-room library in Marrero we can look out the window at mimosa and oleander planted among the typical "shotgun" houses of this Southern region.   Inside, a group of parochial school girls are checking out books with near-religious zeal, but nothing strikes us as uniquely Southern.   We drive on, through the flatlands, past a thousand backyard banana palms, and arrive at the Charles A. Wagner

Private arms are big in the South, and this young man at the Wagner Branch tells us, "I've read about every war there ever was."

Branch, busiest in the system.   The neighborhood is affluent,
manicured.   In fact, almost everything we observe inside and
outside the library at Wagner seems as if it were produced
for a USIA film on the good life in America.   The library
building is attached to a fire house with merry red engines.
There are pro-Nixon signs all over the place for tomorrow's
election; kids wear "USA" shirts, and patriotic books are on
display.   There are Southern touches--a sprig of cotton on a
shelf and a boy reading a book about guns.   (Private arms
are big in the South, especially in this area, Walsh confides.)

Even though the boy with the book is more interested
in martial history than in rooftop sniping, it is less than re-
assuring.

"I've read about every war there ever was," he tells
us.

But library life goes on in Jefferson Parish.   It will
go on very smoothly, indeed, with the certain leadership of
Mr. Walsh--a reserve colonel,[12] with a human side in reserve.

A Run through the Black Belt

We have sneaked up on Mississippi in the dark of
night.   The slimy waters of the Gulf are menacing; the sand
beaches glow an eerie, moon-yellow.   Tomorrow is Election
Day, 1972.   We had thought, in our naïveté, that a Yankee
journalist ought not to be snooping around in deepest Dixie on
a day when personal, perhaps vehement political feelings are
to be expressed.   But we resolve with some anxiety as we
go to sleep that we are going to snoop anyway.

Tomorrow creeps in, and with it the prosaic reality
of tribal America--one great consumer group of network TV,

national brands, and interstate highways--and as we move
slowly through Gulfport, Miss., it couldn't matter less who
we are or what day it is. On the surface, life (and library
life) is going on as it usually does, which is much the same
as it does elsewhere in the States. We cross a little moat
over a pond of lily pads, and we enter the Gulfport-Harrison
County Library. We have come without warning, and we are
free to pursue the Southern mystique and mystery beneath the
smooth, sun-bathed flow of daily library life. At first, we
detect nothing.

But we do feel an apprehension in the air. Of course,
there is always a general apprehension on Election Day, as
one contemplates the crises of the next four years, military,
economic, educational, or whichever; but we are also on the
site of nature's famous 1969 assault on the South's educational resources: Hurricane Camille. The librarians of Gulfport-Harrison, in particular, will never forget the day of
August 17 in that year, when Camille smashed ruthlessly
through the huge windows of their beautiful, three-year-old
library building, set like a precious white stone just above
the open beach, and destroyed some 40,000 books and many
other irreplaceable items. The aftermath is legend, with
many grim details. (A dead dog was found washed up near
a book entitled "Be Kind to Animals.") Maria Person, a
beloved librarian who had already devoted the best energy of
her life to this library, is said to have died from the strain
--night and day--of trying to restore it from the shambles
of that August.

Today it is once again a showplace--a modern villa
on the sea--and one with a relatively threadbare operating
budget. The old story! The community, out of pride, demands a first-rate physical plant, even raises the money

locally, but cannot sustain, cannot comprehend the need for, services to match.   Thus, one enters the graceful, airy lobby of the building, pauses in the sweet smell of a butterfly lily near the well furnished children's room--but finds no children's librarian.   No young adults' librarian.   An attractive, honey-voiced reference librarian has been on the job for ten years and, although she has no library degree, serves the community of 134,000 apparently as well as is needed. But elsewhere the lack of professional librarians will tell.

It is not only a matter of attitude; it is hard to attract good professionals and to hold them on Southern salaries, especially in a State with no accredited library school.

There is a school library next door, but it closes at three.   What school activity can compete with the Southern-style manias of football and marching bands?   There were also black branches at one time, but now the library is integrated and we see blacks using the collections, including a scattering of reading materials of black interest.

Earlier in the day, an electric storm that made our hair stand up as straight as sticks darkened the skies, then fled; it reminded us that nature is capricious in this region and can perform as oddly and outrageously without a moment's notice as, say, a national administration.   And the librarians here can be as apprehensive about the one as the other.   With such a small operating budget now, further cuts in library funds could be as devastating as another Camille.

We leave this uneasy site, and travel through pine forests on a highway to Hattiesburg, home of Southern Mississippi University and its library.   Ah yes, the groves of academe will comfort us again, for the 8,000 students at SMU are a mild-mannered bunch, no trouble, a moderately integrated population, a great many of them here to become

Southern Mississippi University Librarian Warren Tracy
among the papers of Theodore G. Bilbo, state governor and
U.S. Senator.

educators. There are some charming old buildings on the
campus, the old library among them. But the new library--
neo-warehouse in design--is merely spacious, accommodating,
devoid of scholarly ambience. Chief Librarian Warren Tracy
is doing what he can toward building the collection into something worthy of university scholarship--for the library served
only a college until 1962, when university status was granted
and Dr. Tracy came to Hattiesburg from Indiana by way of
Louisiana. A Mississippian is making the task as painless
as possible for him: University President William D. Mc-
Cain, whom Dr. Tracy calls the "most library-minded administrator I've ever known."

Among the materials being acquired are those to support black studies in the school, but there are no black li-

brarians on the staff to specialize in these or any other acquisitions.   Dr. Tracy tells us that he has had only one ap-
plication from a black librarian, who then chose to work
elsewhere.

We see plenty of black students using the library on
this afternoon, however, and several working as library aides.
There is no sign that there was ever a strain between black
and white students working closely together in this capacity,
or that there might once have been irony in a black aide dis-
pensing Mississippi historical and genealogical materials to
a white student.

We leave the building impressed that Dr. Tracy, a
laconic but gracious interviewee, is a dedicated Southern librarian, that the collections--especially rich in the papers of
such prominent Mississippians as Governor and U. S. Senator
Theodore G. Bilbo--are admirable, but that the library lacks
the excitement of some of the Northern university libraries
we have seen (oh, we've seen some dreary ones up there,
too).   We query one last student in regard to the "spirit of
the library," if any, that he perceives, and he snorts so
vigorously at the idea of "spirit" and "library" in the same
breath that he has to wipe his nose.

Books Fell on Alabama

It is another day, another State, another type of library.   We find ourselves--again unannounced--at the George
C. Wallace Junior College and Technical Institute in Alabama
on our way to the Selma-Montgomery Route across the State.

Now who is George C. Wallace?   It may come as a
surprise to those who thought he had done little else as Governor but block college doors that he is something of a patron

saint for the thousands of students at the eighteen junior colleges established since he first turned his attention to this area of education in 1963, and for the teachers and librarians employed therein. Wallace was determined that the State-supported junior colleges, with open admissions, should be first-rate in every respect, and a visit to this newest of his JCS seems to bear out his commitment.

The librarian is a professional, and a good one. He is a modest Southerner from Tennessee named William Buchanan: library degree from LSU, prior experience in college and school libraries. He shows us through what appears to be an adequate facility for the 750 students, but we learn that it is only a temporary facility, and that the new library on the drawing board will be three times as classy. He admits that he was attracted to junior college librarianship partly because the salary is better than that for Alabama university librarians below the department-head level, but now into the job, he loves it. "It's a teaching thing," he explains. "I do as much teaching as the faculty." There are students of all levels here: bright, slow, poor, rich. Some who could have gotten into and afforded prestigious colleges simply don't want to leave home to do so. Buchanan works closely with the students and provides remedial help when necessary, as it often is. He is building up the resources with the help of Bertalan's The Junior College Library Collection. So are most of his Alabaman library colleagues, a close-knit fraternity. (It continually surprises us how Southern librarians all seem to know one another.) Eventually he will hire another professional librarian, and they will both have to take at least six hours of post-master's professional training every two years to keep up with the standards for Alabama's State JC librarians.

The students we talk to have high praise for the library and librarian. They tell horror stories of their high school libraries and seem turned on about learning how to use a real one.

Buchanan agrees that the number of blacks in the school--about ten percent--is low considering that about sixty percent of this Selma region is black. He feels, though, that things are moving; his young student aides, particularly the black aides, eagerly took advantage of time allotted for voting yesterday. And the Selma City Council has three blacks out of seven members.

Certainly, this last development is a far cry from the cries in the night not so very long ago. A friendly Selma resident in front of the Selma Public Library a little later

Selma citizen, pickup truck, and Carnegie Library. On the surface, things haven't changed much in recent years, but the library was integrated well before Dr. King's Selma-Montgomery march.

offers to show us the very tree nearby on which townsfolk
lynched the last victim.

The public library in Selma goes back almost a hundred years, and the present building, serving a city and
county population of about 50,000, dates from 1908. There
are no branches, no bookmobiles, and the central library,
gateway to self-improvement, is about as inviting as an old
bus terminal. The city now has some $1.5 million in HUD
funds, and it must decide whether to build a library or an
auditorium with it in a new civic center. Otherwise, there
is no other library building money in sight. [13]

The librarian, Patricia Blalock, is a youthful and extremely pleasant Alabaman whose long years of residence in
Selma (40), of library service (25), and library directorship
(12) do not seem to weigh on her bright, energetic bearing
as she welcomes the unexpected visitor and shows him around.
She has no library degree--she was a social worker--but she
has what we have time and again noted in our travels to be
the most valuable professional asset at the public service
level--knowledge of her clientele. She has desk assistants,
but, "It's important for me to spend time at the desk, also.
That's where I come to know the people and what they want."

"The people" in the library have included blacks for
some time now; it was integrated well before the historic
march of Dr. King, and there are black-related materials on
the shelves and racks.

We leave the library, inspired by the fortitude of Mrs.
Blalock in serving so many so cheerfully for so long in such
dreary facilities. From whence she draws her strength is
not as immediately obvious as it is with a patron who enters
as we leave. She is a sinewy young woman with blonde hair
in long curls, and the bike from which he has just leapt with

a vengeance bears the huge sign: GOD IS MY CO-PILOT.

Selma to Montgomery

The spirit of Martin Luther King touches us as we
speed coolly along the route of the long, hot march, and we
stop only to gather a little dried-out cotton in a field near
the road. We are in the Black Belt of the South, a term
that refers to the color of the soil and not population ratios.
Of course, black soil is for cotton, and cotton brought black
slaves and workers.

Montgomery's soil gives rise to the Governor's Man-
sion, the State Capitol, and other notable buildings, among
them the ten-year-old Main Library: an appealing, well used,
and already-too-small brick structure.   Its aesthetic appeal
is enhanced by an attractive director from California, Mary
Haas.

With a business background and a library degree
earned only in 1970, Mrs. Haas has had little time to be
swallowed up either by the "professional" library mystique
or the Southern mystique, such as it exists, and she is not
afraid to talk freely.

"The South's problems as I've found them are so ...
subterranean.   Things are done differently [than in the West
and Southwest]; they move a little slowly ... the relationships are more personal, intimate.   You deal in politics,
grass roots, every day of your life....   Everyone belongs
to something in the community and works hard at it.

"... No, we haven't had censorship problems.   ...
There's a strong religious influence that's reflected in our
having a Young People's Collection [moral and religious literature especially written for youth] and maybe a lack of the

literary sophistication that would make such a special collection unnecessary."

The library, with two branches and a bookmobile,
serves 147,000 in the city and walk-in patrons of three or
four counties. The staff of forty has only two professional
librarians. Some 154,000 titles are in the collection, "but
there's not enough money to do anything in AV."

Federal money is something of a novelty for the Montgomery PL, but only because of certain prior circumstances.
Mrs. Haas detects no resistance among Southerners to federal money. "Everyone scrambles for it!"

Unlike the Selma PL, Montgomery does not serve the
private schools, most of which are segregated. But it
reaches out to the public schools--most grade schools have
no library--to the elderly, to pre-school children, and to the
retarded, among others.

... Here's to You, Dr. Robinson

From MPL we phone ahead to our next destination,
Alabama State University across town, where we will have
our first talk with a Southern black librarian at a black Southern school and library.

The librarian is Dr. Harry Robinson, and we are almost dumbfounded as we enter his office. There, seated
with cool confidence at a huge desk, hands folded, sizing us
up, is a young man we had noticed a few days ago in the
lobby of the Jung Hotel in New Orleans, a man we had hoped
to interview about being a black librarian in the Deep South,
but who had seemed almost too shy to be approached.

Dr. Robinson's credentials are awesome for one so
young. His library degree is from Atlanta; he has a Cer-

Harry Robinson at Alabama: "I want to contribute something to the brothers ... and I can do that best in the South."

tificate of Advanced Study in Librarianship from the University of Illinois in addition to a doctorate in instructional technology and library science. He has done additional study in librarianship at Wayne State and Miami University in Ohio. He has worked as cataloger, documents librarian, instructor, and college librarian. Now dean of Learning Resources at Alabama State, he is what might be called a highly marketable librarian, even in these lean times. Yet, no Southern white universities have come after him--only one college which he, as a black, was unable to attend when he was ready for college in his home State of Louisiana. ("Instead, my father almost starved himself to death to send me through Southern University.") The college offered him a job, "but why should I have gone there to help them fill a quota or meet some regulation for federal funding?"

There were offers from "white" schools in the North, but these, too, he turned down.

Warming to us now, friendly, communicative, he confides that, "it may sound racist, but right now I don't want to work at a white school. I'm a Christian, I try to love ... but I'm still haunted by too many memories." He tells us a story of a white woman he had worked for as a youth, and how she would put her dog in the front seat, Harry in the back, when she drove her car.

"But I want to contribute something to the brothers, too," he adds, "and I can do that best in the South ... here."

He has a mission at Alabama State, where there is much to be done in bringing together the 3,200 students and 125,000 books and other media in a way that will be meaningful and that will avoid duplication of services elsewhere in the university. The black materials--still "integrated" into the collection or under "N" for Negro--will be segregated,

partly as an inducement for getting them used. "We have to
pull all the tricks we can." Staff members (there are five
professional librarians) with no black-school experience must
be "re-educated," and the stacks and special collections must
be kept open. "If accessibility to materials were as hard for
me as it has been for students, I'd do some mutilating, too."

There is good support from the administration and
faculty, good beginnings of cooperation with other libraries
in the area.

Even though it is supper hour, we see a number of
students racing from catalog to circulation desk, making the
kinds of demands on the collection that are every library
school student's dream of what the academic experience might
yield; now, all that idealist/realist Harry Robinson has to do
is to deliver, and his "black experience" in Southern Library
Life will be a happy one.

Booktrucking in the 'bama Boonies

        We are ready to go about as deep as a body can go
in the Deep South and still find library services: into the
backwoods, the boondocks of the Tallapoosa River. We are
traveling out of Dadeville, the Tallapoosa County seat, with
a population that would barely fill the Library of Congress
reading rooms. In much of this country the sky is blocked
out by the thickness of the pines, and the undergrowth is
strangled and covered over with kudzu vine. Other parts,
however, are simply the rural South as many Yankees imagine
it: a black-top highway with red-dirt shoulders running past
dilapidated shacks; folks rocking on porches under tin roofs;
battered pick-up trucks in the driveways; wrecked Fords and
ancient washing machines in the front yards; scraggly hounds

Then, through the windshield of the Horseshoe Bend Regional Library Bookmobile, we see--can it be? "Yes, a black servant is carrying a stack of books to the truck for the white mistress of the house, who comes forth a moment later, empty-handed, to make a selection that the maid will tote back."

barking after you. We are on just such a road now in a Horseshoe Bend Regional Library Gerstenslager bookmobile. Ralph Dodson is at the wheel. His wife, Dettie, rides circulation desk. They are Alabaman through and through, and have been working on the bookmobile for no less than twenty-one years.

They recall for us how things have changed in that time. First there was a WPA county library in a wood shack. Then a bookmobile you worked from the outside. There were shelves in the truck, but the books would fly out on every turn. Just a few books anyway, nothing for kids.

The bookmobile goes wherever one or more people

are willing to set up a station.   You hope for a large group
at each stop, but it's often just the resident of the station
and sometimes not even he.   Our first stop, for instance,
is up a long red-dirt road to an ancient farmhouse.   An old
man lives alone here, we are told; he can't get out much
and reads about every book they can beg, borrow, or steal
for him.   But we pull up into the yard, and only the hounds
run out at us and raise a racket.   No one emerges from the
shadows of the old, wooden, weather-beaten porch.

The Dodsons move on, a little anxious over the man's
unusual absence.   They take the bookmobile to another type
of stop entirely: a suburban-style home, with a small swim-
ming pool in the back and big Detroit iron in the driveway.
Only the resident of the house comes on board, half-hearted-
ly taking some books for her children--who have access to
other library materials--and joking about a teacher who, get
this, voted for McGovern on Tuesday.

The next stop is even more surprising for what we
expected from a backwoods bookmobile.   We look past Ralph
out the side window and see a plantation-style porch with
white pillars suitable for an ante bellum backdrop, and then,
through the windshield--can it be?   Yes, a black servant is
carrying a stack of books to the truck for the white mistress
of the house, who comes forth a moment later, empty-handed,
to make a selection that the maid will tote back.   Glory be!
Are we trapped in a time warp?

We know that a librarian alone cannot bring her patrons into the twentieth century, but we are surprised to find
any element less than humane and contemporary in a system
run by Kathleen Imhoff.   For some time now, ever since she
won a John Cotton Dana library publicity award, we have
tuned an ear to Mrs. Imhoff's work in the Deep South, and,

for a Wisconsin-reared liberal in this rural territory, she
has had several impressive victories.   Then why does she
permit tax-supported bookmobiles to serve those who are
hardly willing to serve themselves upon being serviced?

We can ask her directly, for she has met the bookmobile here, bringing a car in which we will visit a few "urban" libraries in the system during the afternoon.

Kathleen smiles at our question much as a war-tough-
ened old vet might grin at a green recruit just arriving at

Kathleen Imhoff at the Horseshoe Bend Regional Library she
ran in Alabama's backwoods country.

the front who asks: "Why don't we attack in broad daylight?"
Of course, instead of to a leathery sergeant we are talking
to an exceptionally beautiful and brilliant woman of twenty-
six. But she was just a kid of twenty-two when she arrived
in Alabama, and she had some fancy green ideas herself a-
bout making changes. She and her husband Clement, a teacher, were and are humanitarian idealists with missionary energy, and although they operate with a firm but light touch
now, Kathleen came on a little too strong for an outsider
when she arrived and had her wrists slapped more than once.
There was plenty to upset her: blacks had to stand outside
of bookmobiles at one time; story hours were segregated (she
still has trouble with certain churches which will not allow a
black story-teller to operate on their premises); in some instances, blacks were being refused books on the grounds that
they do not bring them back (Kathleen took statistics and
proved that the notion was absolutely false). Even when Kathleen won the Dana award, there was flak: "First she accepts
out-of-State recognition, then she goes all the way to Chicago
to claim it!"

     It must not be misconstrued, however, that life at the
regional headquarters in Dadeville is unpleasant. The LSCA
building (1968) is modern and comfortable; the collection of
125,000 volumes is lovingly selected and up to date (virtually
no censorship); the Dadeville Public Library, in the same
building, provides a pleasant and knowledgeable neighbor in
librarian Louise Oliver; many others of the system staff and
trustees are a pleasure to know. But there are still enough
frustrations to make a Yankee a little more homesick each
day. In the branches, for instance, certain sins of library
service take place which are entirely out of Kathleen's control.

We visit some of these branches on our afternoon tour. The first is in a mill town named Alexander City; thanks to the benevolent aid and controlling interests of the mill boss's wife, the building is a huge, posh, indestructible mausoleum with antique furniture (e. g., 18th-century Chippendale)--but with 5,000 books for 12,000 citizens, no shelving space for any more, no posters, no audiovisuals (a few records kept in a closet), no circulation to speak of, and, not long ago, no blacks allowed at story hours.

Elsewhere in the system, a new branch being built for the Goodwater community offers more hope of being a please-touch, please-use facility. The present one is a storefront branch on a dreary main street right out of The Last Picture Show. The librarian, well beyond retirement age, is dedicated, but the winds of Southern-small-town life and tradition seem to waft her more toward serving the town's white academy than the public and predominantly-black high school. Yet, she tries her best to give service where it's needed, and the new branch will be good news. In the past, library funds were solicited from the town's fifty percent black population as well as from the white half, but later there was some hesitation in giving full service to the blacks. That was the bad news.

If and when Kathleen leaves Dadeville, certain aspects of library life will go on in a forward-moving direction as they did before she arrived: book stock, circulation, and budget, for instance, have risen steadily since 1940. But Mrs. Imhoff, who also runs what is probably the only women's consciousness-raising group in the whole Tallapoosa Valley, is a brave human being and a professional who has brought some library-service-consciousness to a few who were eager to have it--and a few who were not. She has made a difference.

Full Circle: A Southern School Library

We have come the full circle.   We are face-to-pretty-
face with the Southern school librarian who told us on the
phone a week earlier that we would not overcome our Yankee
biases.   But we have traveled so far in such a short time
that we feel we have been living the Southern library life for
years; we are suddenly surprised to refer to ourselves as
Yankee as we rehash the question of biases.   Doesn't she detect our Southern accent?

We are in the Central High School Library of Phenix
City, Ala.   Forget about Phenix City as a sin center; that's
all in the dark past, and the major blight now is the industrial
smoke that blows across the Choctawhatchee River from Co-
lumbus, Ga., whose textile mills dominate the skyline.

We were drawn to Phenix City by a paper written by
Central Librarian Patricia McCain and by Sharon Williamson,
then a teacher at the school.   It was a study of circulation
data gathered from 1968 through 1972, the years surrounding
the integration of Phenix Central.   "Integration has stirred
up many questions to be debated, among them the feeling that
because many Black students had received instruction inferior
to that of the white students there would be an adverse influence on the white students' future instruction."   What the
study found, however, was merely a subject shift that would
require "further research ... in order to establish more
clear-cut conclusions."   The shift was a circulation rise in
biographies, religion, social science, language, pure and applied science, and literature; and a decrease in fiction, art,
history, and geography.

Statistically, it is a modest, limited study, but it has
led us to a librarian who cares about the true nature of a

In the library of Phenix, Ala., Central High School. The students tend to sit apart, by race, as they do in the North. But they do enjoy the library itself; at least they're not yet turned off.

changing library audience and how best to serve it. Of
course, for the forty percent black population now in the
school, she is spending most of her library money on the
collection--buying almost everything she can find of black interest. "The main problem is finding good black fiction."
She is, admittedly, a bit lagging in securing AV materials of
black interest, and a little reluctant to segregate black materials from others in the collection. The students segregate
themselves in their library seating patterns--just as they do
in most Northern schools--and collection segregation might
seem to be additionally divisive.

Pat McCain is still feeling her way around, since integration at Central is only two years old and fairly recent
in general. She grew up not long ago nearby in Alabama,
and as a white child of her time never attended school with
blacks. She feels that she was never really bigoted, but that
the racial line of which she was so conscious is gradually
disappearing. She tells us--and we see, from some late afternoon visitors--that she has an easy friendship with several
of the black teachers on the staff. About half her student
aides are black, working for an elective credit, and we observe an instance of good rapport with them: a library aide
from last year, a Central graduate, is doing a Thanksgiving
program for her church, and drops in for resources on program planning. She had already been to the local library,
didn't find anything, and came back to a librarian she trusts.

But perhaps we are making snap judgments. Anyway,
there is more to a Southern school library than the black-
white challenge, and Mrs. McCain has many other concerns.
She is securing materials on drugs, although she confesses
to feeling a little awkward in dealing with resources on VD
and other sex-education topics. Other frustrations and satis-

factions: the Library Club is very weak; the principal is library minded (his wife is a librarian). Finally, one of the
highest satisfactions: the students, without raising hell, are
having a good time in the library. Phenix Central has a
population of 800, and includes only 11th and 12th grades, so
that the library user is likely to be a little more mature than
in the larger, more inclusive secondary schools. But to put
it in the most basic terms, we have been to happy school libraries; we have been to sad ones. Perhaps the students of
Phenix Central are not yet turned on to the potential of a
living, loving, media resource center; perhaps the school
has not yet created one; but at least the students are not yet
turned off, and the staff has the will to find the way.

Yes, Howard ... yes, Patricia ...

And so, the full circle ended, we drive through Georgia into Atlanta. We look back on our week in the Deep
South and reflect: yes, Howard Zinn, library life there is
more a mirror image of the best and worst up North than
part of an unfathomable mystique; and, yes, Patricia McCain,
we could not, cannot, leave our Yankee biases in New York.
But at least we came to see, and we looked, and what we
saw became a part of us. And now we wonder as we return
to the cruel, hostile shores of the Bronx and some of its un-
disciplined, unfriendly libraries--can we leave our Southern
biases behind?

Chapter Seven

The West Coast Style and the
Search for the Great American Library Dream

It had been ages since I'd been on the West Coast long enough
to get the feel of it. I had lived there only for a summer as
a teenager. It was 1956. I wrote my share of American
Graffiti then, chasing convertibles down Sunset Strip and into
all-night drive-ins, and by days I took a sleepy little part in
the booming American economy, drilling holes in DC-7s at
the Douglas plant in Santa Monica. One day, when the planes
were too crowded with electricians for us mechanics to enter,
I walked the seemingly endless production line, took some
turns, and came upon a hangar in which I was allowed an
astonishing glimpse of the future: there, sparkling in sun-
beams and put together like a brand new model airplane, was
the prototype DC-8, just about the biggest and slickest thing
I'd ever seen.

Now, in 1974, I was boarding what looked to me like
an antiquated old buzzard for my flight to the West Coast
from New York, and when I sat down and heard the stewardess
say it was a DC-8, it gave me pause.

Clearly, what little I had known from experience about
the Real West Coast was now faded or outdated, and my only
other conceptions of it were based on pop literature, confer-
ence-burdened business trips, and a few brief, mindless vaca-

154

tion days. I realized I was moving through the same cloud
of unknowing as on other departing flights for this journal,
and again I pored desperately through background materials.
For the outsider's view can be a useful one, provided he is
not so naïve, his stereotypes and mythologies not so fixed,
that Truth flees at his approach.

Two and a half weeks later, by the time I completed
the assignment, I at least knew the difference between Sutter,
Sutro, Seattle, and the Sierras, and some of my most stereotyped preconceptions had been shattered. But never, in all
my travels and interviews from Puget Sound to Disneyland,
did I abandon the search for a salient West Coast style, particularly as it might appear in libraries.

Libraries, after all, reflect the lifestyle of people,
librarians included. We know something about how libraries
correspond or don't correspond to ethnic or economic-group
lifestyles, and we explore further to better understand our
profession. But a regional approach--a search for generalizations, patterns and similarities, as well as for particulars
and differences--not only encompasses ethnic and economic
factors, but adds another dimension to our understanding of
American library life and where it is going.

Some of these thoughts were behind my quest for the
great West Coast library experience.

Did I find it?

Yes and no.

Had I failed utterly, it would not have been the fault
of the West Coast librarians. Familiar with the rest of my
odyssey and amused by my insistence on local color, most
did everything possible to keep me happy. If I asked for a
library on the ocean, I was whisked there within an hour; if
I knew that a librarian sometimes dressed Western, I'd de-

mand and get the full costume for my camera; when I sought
a library reflecting West Coast affluence, the red carpet
rolled out in the richest little community in the nation; if I
called for something unique to the West, I was taken to a
wine library, the Disney Archives, or a library in a redwood
forest; and if I asked for a look at poverty, West Coast style,
my hosts tried their best (though what I saw of these library
patrons we would call "middle class" in the East, and the
neighborhoods, "Easy Street").

　　But did I find the Great West Coast Library Experience?

　　The rest of this chapter is my answer.   It is meant
to be less a portrait of individual libraries than a mural of
interlocking themes.   But perhaps we can step back for just
a moment to pick out a few highlights and overall impres-
sions:

　　West Coast libraries depend on federal money as much
as do libraries everywhere.   In general, where these funds
had dried up, we found library survival; where they were
available, we found library _life_.

　　West Coast libraries are more a cultural blend than we
have seen elsewhere.   Many ethnic patterns are embraced as
part of the still-forming West Coast style.   In a black-neigh-
borhood branch in San Francisco, an Anglo boy borrows Asian
children's books; in the Chinatown Branch, the black children's
librarian presented a popular program of African dancers; a
backwoods library in Washington State features "authentic"
Kwakiutl Indian designs painted into its beautiful rough-wood
walls.   They were done by a white man; but the branch's
white librarian has, in turn, adopted a Kwakiutl boy who
teaches her about his heritage.   In an entirely Spanish-speaking neighborhood of Los Angeles, the recently appointed black

branch librarian can't yet speak the language (she's studying it), yet she runs her library well: "She understands people," said a staff member, "and she knows when to delegate authority to her Spanish-speaking community aides." Taking photos in a Seattle school library, we could have picked almost any table to represent the mingling of three or four races (and no one could agree on whose particular life style dominates the school; at the time, the toughest kids were some of those just coming from the slums of Manila, but the school president is Filipino--and so it goes).

In every region visited, funds were cited as the greatest problem in library life, not censorship, not library use.

Librarians there are a mixed lot, some freaky, some West Coast chic (as we envisioned it), others traditional

West Coast library life: a cultural blend. At Franklin High School in Seattle, "we could have picked almost any table to represent three or four races." Standing is librarian Earle Johnson; on his left, School President Darrel Mamallo from the Philippines.

Highly competent Spanish-speaking aides help the Lincoln Heights Branch, LAPL, relate to its community.

At the busy, black Watts branch of Los Angeles Public, which
some outsiders still envision as a trouble spot, the atmosphere could not be more pleasant. Branch Librarian Ida
Davis, above, stressed that there is no lower vandalism rate
in the LAPL system.

Marians, straight as school marms and masters. They don't all love their jobs, but by and large they mean to stay put in them because the market is airtight and they don't want to leave the region and their groovy homes. But the discontented don't stew all day; they balance out their lives with their own thing: a little shop, a craft, an independent information service, volunteer outreach, or they simply dip into the great West Coast outdoor natural organic spiritual self-realization grab bag and come up revitalized.

The most shocking vandalism we saw was in a white suburb near Seattle: $1,600 worth of windows smashed in a beautiful new branch. The most surprising tale of juvenile crime, which is spreading throughout the Coast, concerned teachers in one of the richest Bay Area school districts who had to lock classroom doors from the inside because of gang raids during the day. At the busy, black Watts branch of Los Angeles, however, which some outsiders still envision as a trouble spot, the atmosphere could not be more sedate, and there is no lower vandalism rate in the LAPL system.

There are accredited library schools galore on the Coast, pumping out professionals about as useful in a tight market as raw sewage. True, some systems are expanding: King County in Washington has built sixteen new branches since 1966. But in others, there is implosion, not growth.

In Los Angeles, it's been ten years since the city opened the doors of a new public library building, and some 75 school librarians provide service for more than 400 elementary schools. Orange County's Anaheim City District is up to something even more frightening to dyed-in-the sheepskin professionals. With Title II money, it has established 21 media-packed Comprehensive Learning Centers--super libraries--in its elementary schools. But now, so they can be

staffed on district funds, it is a "library technician" who heads
each one, with a two-year associate degree in library science
or a bachelor's in anything.   They work for pay between that
of aides and teachers, and everyone seems satisfied with the
quality of service.   As it happens, there are a few who hold
library degrees and still work at the sub-faculty pay rate.
That's how eager people are to keep living in this winterless
wonderland.   And it isn't just California.   As one Seattle
school-librarian-turned-media-teacher put it, "This is the
only place I could be for where my life is."   How can you
argue with that?

Sometimes you can find local color in the circulation
patterns.   At the Seattle Public Library, for instance: "Last
year, during the gold rush, all the books on panning went out.
And you can tell when Boeing is hiring--out go the books on
welding."   In Los Angeles, too, a big rush on gold maps and
mining and panning literature at the central library.   At the
library of King Co. (Wash.) Youth Service Center, a deten-
tion facility with a large percentage of runaways: "We seem
to have a heavy interest in maps of nearby States."   From
North Hollywood: "A constant and overwhelming demand for
materials on exorcism."   And from the 200,000 Mormons in
L.A.:   a religiously-motivated use of genealogical materials.
In practically every West Coast library, of course, there are
never-ending demands for crafts, outdoor recreation, alternative living, and automotive materials.   In Bellevue, Wash.,
every item in the library's big collection circulates freely,
save one group: the auto manuals, which must be requested.
"They're impossible!"   And at both the Bay Area Reference
Center's downtown San Francisco headquarters and the Carnation (pop. 600) Public Library in the Washington wilderness,
The Mother Earth News is just about the most valuable source

Librarian David Smith and, above him, the man whose archives he watches over in Burbank, California.

for alternative, grow-your-own info.

But library local color is more than materials and their use. For your browsing pleasure, we present a little gallery of vignettes:

Isolated Splashes of Color in a Panoramic View of Library Life on the West Coast

"The old Seattle Public Library was the only library building in the country you could enter through the restrooms."

The newspaper vault in the catacombs of L.A.'s central library building is called the oy ge-vault for the headaches it represents. Nearby is an infamous, dark, twisting storage corridor named Rat Alley.

Youthful offenders benefit from library materials in the King County (Wash.) Youth Service Center, but try telling that to police who recently busted a kid on pot charges. With him he had a book he'd taken from the Center library: Pot Shots.

"The Bellevue [Wash.] Public Library is banning books!" a citizen told the local newspaper. An investigation turned up something slightly different: an exhibit of books that had been banned through the ages.

An L.A. architectural critic called the central library the city's "one salient historical building." But a scholar has cataloged some 50 historical mistakes in the noted History Room murals by Albert Herter.

A librarian who ejected a mother because her daughter was too heavy a library user? Yes, in Newport Way, Wash. First, the mother belted the 2-year-old off her lap. In return, the daughter proceeded to tear the library apart--which seemed fair enough to the mother, but not to the librarian, who gave her the thumb.

Librarian David R. Smith of the Disney Archives in Burbank has two special preservation problems: people and termites. The former are Disney Studio workers who used to feed Disney "trash" to a paper shredder before the Archives could get a look at it for memorabilia; and the latter are fond of eating the graphic lines on the original animation drawings for Disney cartoons. The archives has 50 million such drawings!

According to Carl Cox of the San Francisco Public Library,
the first readers to freak on The Exorcist were men in the
county prisons, to whom he helps bring library materials.

What kind of issues concern a West Coast social responsibilities group? For the Washington (State) Library Association SRRT, it is racism against the Japanese. Because there
are so many citizens of Japanese descent in the State, one
recent SRRT protest is against the term "Jap" as an abbrevi-
ation of Japan or Japanese in Webster's New Collegiate Dic-
tionary.

Many readers call the Huntington Library in Pasadena a para-
dise, a garden of Eden, and indeed some of the grounds a-
round it make Kew Gardens look sparse. Little wonder that
one reader has been coming in since 1940 for work on his
topic ("The Negro in California"), and that others have been
working on research projects there since the mid '30s. The
library's 300,000 rare books, 200,000 reference volumes, its
priceless, lovingly acquired manuscripts, and gracious treat-
ment of readers might have something to do with it, too.

At another paradisiacal setting, Malaga Cove, Calif., the library occupies a Spanish-style villa overlooking the sea and
features such amenities as a bowl of fresh petals on the circulation desk. But each day it is harassed by a neighbor who
shrieks and struts and who has never read a work in his life.
Yet, the librarians tolerate it; for who can tell a peacock not
to do his thing?

The sole library survivor of the 1906 San Francisco earth-
quake and fire was a portion of Adolph Sutro's private col-
lection--less than half of his original 300,000 volumes, then
the largest private library in the land. Today the Sutro Library is a free, public branch of the Calif. State Library,
housed in the (Jesuit) University of San Francisco and run by
author, librarian, and authentic Westerner Richard H. Dillon.
Its specialities are American, English, and Mexican local history and genealogy (or "intimate history," as Dillon prefers),
and researchers come from everywhere to use its rare volumes. Dillon notes a tremendous growth in historical interests, especially on the part of Californians, so many of
whom, he agrees, "are rootless. They have boats, but no
voting address. Now they're interested in setting roots, in
finding regional identity. Every library and bookstore is into
Californiana. Ethnic groups are trying to get out genealogical
works. The shame of American national affairs [Watergate]

is inspiring a search for pride in personal heritage." In the
meantime, Dillon himself is searching for book funds. His
acquisitions budget: about $7,000, enough for a handful of
rare books. Funds for operations and equipment are no better. He keeps his Hebrew scrolls in dynamite boxes.

One photograph we didn't take: a young San Franciscan studying a public library exhibit on the city's Old First Church--
while rolling himself a joint.

At the charming Silverado Museum in St. Helena, Calif.,
there's a Robert Louis Stevenson archive directed by a well
known, "retired" rare books librarian of the Free Library of
Philadelphia, Ellen Shaffer. Giving out brochures at the door
is a retired dean of Mills College. They have a ball there,
in the heart of the wine country.

In Palos Verdes' enormously popular library, some patrons
have asked if they could be married in the building's multi-
purpose room. The request was denied only because the
room was booked too far in advance.

Inside the Huntington Library, Pasadena. Some readers have
stayed for forty years.

Librarian and Western historian Richard H. Dillon, watched
over by Adolph Sutro, whose private library has grown into
a major research collection in San Francisco. Mr. Dillon
runs it for the State Library.

The Great Dream

When you write of the West Coast, its libraries or anything
else about it, sooner or later the great clichés about the last
frontier, the American dream, the American future, Eldorado,
or the westering urge start beating at the windows of the
prose until you have to let a few in the front door.   After
all, the librarians do talk about the Coast as the place from
which they can go no further, and many latecomers to it project a sense of triumph over their Eastern or Midwestern origins.   It isn't just California; several in Seattle said that the
trouble is "you never want to leave."   And who in the library
profession elsewhere can say they never looked at those clas-

The sun doesn't always shine at the end of the Western rain-
bow, as this patron of the White Center Library (Seattle)
knows.   But the trouble with this area isn't the rain, according to the natives.   It's that "you never want to leave."

sified ads for jobs in the Bay Area or Carmel or some other
charming Coastal community and never dreamed the great
Westward Ho, New Life, Good Life, sunshiny dream? Time
and again at conferences you hear the table-thumping proclama-
tion, 'I'm just going to go there--I'll find something!" Although few actually go, and fewer find something.

Yet, they talk about it; West Coast patrons read about
it; writers such as San Francisco City Librarian Kevin Starr
write about it; and, of course, to any two librarians it means
two entirely different things. To the black librarian of the
Watts branch, who grew up in Alabama with her professional
opportunities then limited to teaching, the West Coast means
a place where she "can be anything"--even though "for sale"
signs popped up around her newly-purchased home in a nice-
looking neighborhood. To Myra Nadler, who was reared in
Brooklyn, it means a dream library, a dream job in wealthy
Palos Verdes. To the coordinator of children's services at
San Francisco PL, with fonder memories of what she calls
the New York and Cleveland library spirit, "the reality is not
at all like the dream." And when we dreamily asked a member of the Bay Area Reference Center if SFPL is to other libraries as San Francisco is to other cities, the reply was
simply that "San Francisco is not what everyone thinks it is.
What it winds up with is pretty middle of the road."

And, of course, we know about the many dismal fail-
ures and nightmares of West Coast life, the perversions of
the frontier vision. Starr's book focuses on those between
1850 and 1915. Michael Davie's California; the Vanishing
Dream (Dodd, Mead, 1972) is an excellent updating. In Seattle, the dream sometimes turns on the fortunes of Boeing--
and had a fairly seedy beginning, too, according to William
Speidel's Sons of the Profits (Nettle Creek, 1967), a favorite
local history.

But what did West Coast libraries mean to <u>me</u> in
terms of the dream and what I had seen elsewhere for this
journal? In my quest for the great American library experience, did I catch a glimpse of the ideal, or of the future?

Yes, I glimpsed both; and the experience brought to
mind sentiments akin to those expressed by the late Chet
Huntley on his last news broadcast, when he exhorted the
American people to be patient, "for there will be better and
happier news one day if we work at it." In the sphere of
library service, I can't say I saw them work at it any harder
in the West than in Appalachia, the Midwest, the Plains, and
the South; but perhaps because more citizens are using their
libraries in an undespairing pursuit of the good life, because
more librarians are able to bring their own thing to bear
upon library life, the news about what many have called a
dying institution is already beginning to look a little better
on the West Coast.

These, of course, are generalizations I wouldn't even
set out to prove; but at least I can describe some of the particulars that gave rise to the feelings.

The Future Through the Eye of a Needle

Is it because so many people came to Seattle to escape the past that the futuristic is welcomed here as enthusi-
astically as those rare glimpses of the winter sun? Certainly since 1962, when the Seattle World's Fair (Century 21)
brought a number of Tomorrow's elements--such as mono-
rails--into present everyday Seattle life, the city has been
future-minded. Boeing and other modern industries are actually creating the nation's technological future right here on
Puget Sound; and, although there's no lack of sentiment for

the area's colorful, gold-grabbing, lumber-hauling, individual-
istic past, much of the region is taking on a brash modern
look.

It begins for the visitor at the Seattle airport, where
driverless steel shuttle cars whoosh travelers through tubes,
and gentle voices from nowhere lead them to the next auto-
mated device.   And, of course, there's that Space Needle
looming above everything, its elevated saucer a mock flying
object that rules the skies unchallenged.   Not everyone would
want to live in the shadow of such a symbol; but in this area
it is generally accepted.   Here, the future--SSTs and all--is
regarded as the proper business of humanity.   Certainly it
has been the proper business for decades of the King County
Library System, headquartered in a Seattle neighborhood

King County (Washington) Library System has enshrined the
IBM machine that produced in 1950 what was probably the nation's first computerized library book catalog.   A more recent
catalog is also shown, above.

where it looks the Needle right in the eye.

Although the system is run and staffed by plain folk who look nothing at all like the crew of Starship Enterprise, it has already traveled many routes that other libraries only look to in the future:

Its computer-produced book catalog, obviating all card catalogs in the branches, is just about the oldest in the nation (b. 1950), and certainly one of the first to have twenty years' worth of bugs now behind it. Supplemented each week, it works beautifully. You can ask the patrons or the librarians, as we did. The machine that produced the first catalog is now enshrined in the headquarters lobby.

For eight years, the system has had building funds that other systems only dream of, thanks to a $6 million matching library construction bond passed in 1966. The result: sixteen new buildings since that time, several of them organic creations of brick, wood, and glass that Frank Lloyd Wright himself would have been proud to patronize. The interiors are long and sleek and modern, but with warm, natural textures that will enable them to endure stylistically as long as humans value comfort. The Seattle architects, who can so easily take to the forests and rocks and cascading waters for inspiration, are very good indeed. The headquarters building itself is a model for the future on how to refurbish an older structure--in this case, a hangar-sized warehouse. The wood ceilings are refinished, the floors are carpeted, and huge colorful cloth banners break up the great open space of the processing area. It was the first large library processing area I'd ever seen that did not have a factory atmosphere, a great kindness to the workers. The KCLS is kind to its workers in other ways: for instance, there is a real staff development program underway. But even more important, the system is kind to the county citizens, providing the very best of today's and tomorrow's services. For example, while so many American libraries are just now talking about providing some services to local jails, KCLS has been at it for years and doing so well that the county director of public safety could recently say: "Library service is the one public service that residents of King County are offered on the same high level whether they're in jail or out of jail." Every one of the system's million items is available to inmates. At the county youth detention center library, service is so good, the kids so turned on, that some are spoiled for the libraries they'll find in their outside wanderings. And here's the kind of forward-looking service the system provides for its ordinary, popular-book-loving patrons: the "high demand" titles are ordered in appropriate quantity, given a special fast cataloging, and are mailed directly from headquarters to the requester's home, postage free, with no intermediate processing required at the branch.

Naturally, we were shown some of the best elements of the system in our short visit there, but its backward aspects were freely discussed, too. For instance, an affirmative-action hiring program seems due; the staff at every level is mostly paleface (and female). But such a program isn't easy in a system whose minority population is less than four percent of the total. Also, the concept of library-as-community-information-center, as switchboard, hotline for citizen-survival information, represents the future for some librarians around the nation; in KCLS, however, "community information" still means a bulletin board to most branches.

But with patience will come better news, I felt confident. System Director Herbert Mutschler is such a kind soul, giving off such sunny vibes through the winter rains, that ultimately the only harm likely to come out of his administration will be to his personal freedom, for he seems to be utterly consumed by the work and preoccupations of good library service.

Farther away from the Space Needle, but in an area where skyscrapers are beginning to push upward like great fenestrated redwoods, is Future City's central public library building. Neo-Ramada with its glass and bubbly-stone exterior, it was completed in 1959 but still looks slick and modern. Among the users of this library are downtown businessmen and urban young adults, contributing further to the up-to-date look. "The kids change all the time," said a young adult librarian. "Their life styles--very hip. Sometimes they think we're square. They go for 'heady' programs as well as the outdoors-recreation variety." A recent example of the former: a film on future shock.

The Seattle Public Library played a significant part once in the making of future citizens--through Americanization programs, big in the 'twenties. Now there is an increased ethnic consciousness among new immigrants, and the library provides for these interests, too. But in general there is less an attitude of racial separation here than elsewhere, said third-generation Seattleite Julia Owens, head of the Business Section. And in that frantically busy section, where so many members of the different races were working side by side and taking part in the commerce of this space-age metropolis, where a great open body of water and distant mountain ranges out the windows seemed symbolic of unbounded hope and opportunity, we couldn't help having that feeling again: of better news ahead, if we've only got the patience.

Three Dream Libraries;
Other Dreamy Sights

The Seattle Public Library has fifteen branches and
three bookmobiles, a lot going for it. But it has big budget
problems, was facing a $220,000 cut, and lacks AV materials
and other elements of total service. There always seems to
be some tragic flaw to the "perfect" libraries I think I have
uncovered. Through eight years of library journalism, I've
been interested in finding the library that has everything, if
only to see what impact it would have on its community. I
was especially hopeful of picking a winner on this trip to
American Dream country, and chose carefully the candidates
that I would visit.

It was not in vain.

Just south of Los Angeles, a group of hills swoops
dramatically to the ocean to form a peninsula. Four cities
are incorporated within these Palos Verdes Hills, but col-
lectively they are called simply the Hill. About 60,000 people live there. And on the Hill is a library building whose
circulation is third highest in the State after the Los Angeles
and San Francisco central libraries, which serve about three
and one million persons respectively. It is believed that the
per capita circulation of the Palos Verdes District Library (a
main library and two small branches) may be the highest in
the country for a public library system; it is approximately
eighteen per capita. That's one measure of a library's popu-
larity and success; here are some others:

In 1964, a $1,600,000 library bond issue came up,
requiring a fifty-percent affirmative vote for passage. Eighty
percent said yes.

Although the library's annual budget is substantial
about ($1.1 million with some $.2 million for materials), a

At the Palos Verdes District Library, patrons can and do borrow every form of media they could wish for.

taxpayer still called the library the "best bargain on the Hill" for its $.36 tax rate, and apparently other taxpayers agree.

The League of Women Voters named it the Hill's Number One Recreational Facility.

Everyone does it at the library. The Peninsula Center Library (the main branch) seats 250, and it's filled every night. In the four meeting rooms of the three branches, some 1,029 community gatherings were held in '72-73, which is why the library has been unable to find space for those who want to get married on its premises.

Every kind of material circulates, virtually every item; nothing bombs that is bought; every program is a smash.

Why is this library so successful? Money isn't the only answer, though it certainly helps. One of the Peninsula cities, Rolling Hills, has just about the highest per capita income in the nation, some $21,000, and the other three communities aren't exactly slums. It is not an area dominated by the super-rich, who often don't use public libraries; rather, its Mediterranean-style homes are occupied by many well-to-do, well educated professionals: high-level scientists, technologists, and other executives (including the chief librarian of Los Angeles).

An estimated 75 percent of these residents and their families are motivated enough to use the library, compared with about 25 percent across the nation. Mostly liberal Republican, their interests are wide-ranging; only 30 percent of the library's circulation is fiction. The members of the Board also tend to be high-level, educated people--luckily, since it has absolute power over the library. Every so often a group attempts to censor some material, but the community won't have it.

It's a library that has everything for its patrons--

The Palos Verdes District Library has been called the area's "number one recreational facility."

books, AV, projectors, posters, paintings, adult education, Sunday hours, a modern, spacious main library, charming branches, comfortable furnishings, the best equipment--and just about everything for its staff, too: sabbaticals for professionals; a four-day week (36 hours) for all full-timers; long vacations, good fringe benefits, double-time for Sundays, and so on. And that's why it holds a staff that is good enough to keep up with the demand.

At the head of this happy family is a third-generation Angeleno named William Emerson, an unassuming, happy-faced man who once went East for graduate study but probably wouldn't leave his life on the West Coast for all the tea in Boston. (Though you never know.) He traces the good

library life in Palos Verdes back to its origins in 1930, when
75 out of 78 citizens, representing a total of some 500 on
the Hill, voted a $90,000 bond issue for an area library.
Now he has to strain to think of anything that's wrong with
library life here.   "Well," he said, "salaries have leveled
off lately.   We could always use more money."   When asked
about outreach programs, he paused, searching for an honest
answer (he is known as a man of conscience, including in his
role as president of the California Library Association, 1972-
73).   "Frankly," he said, "we just don't know what kinds of
outreach might be valid.   Perhaps shut-in service?   No one
has yet defined a need.   We'll have to make an effort to find
out. "

A second dream library is much like the first, but has
some interesting characteristics of its own.   It's a little wet-
ter, for one thing, being in the Seattle area.
The Bellevue (Wash.) Public Library also serves a-
bout 60,000 eager readers.   Second in the State for a single
library's circulation, it is enjoying such a boom that a second floor is about to be built on top of the spacious, woody,
handsomely furnished first level.   Having a building that was
designed to allow for such expansion is a dream in itself.
It also does some dreamy things for its patrons: Sunday
hours, meeting rooms, clubs, open access to the whole collection.   As part of the King County Library System, it will
arrange for the direct mailing to the patron's home of any
item in the system's catalog.   And the way those book catalogs are used!   Kids who can hardly reach the table whip
through thick computer printouts and find what they want as
easily as ever a child searched the cards.   This library
doesn't condescend to its younger readers.   The entire non-

fiction collection--including reference--is integrated, adult
with children's materials. Unfortunately, the open accessibility has led to a fair number of missing books, not all of
them taken by the John Birchers who were suspected of it
some years ago. There's not much censorship trouble now.

The library has good friends who help provide special
equipment and materials; it has a director, Lynn Lancaster,
who spends "sleepless nights trying to think of innovative programs and services." It is even reported to have had the
first library streaker! But it does not quite have everything:
it and the system are a little slow on AV materials; in a com-
pletely car-oriented suburb, it could use a little more parking space; and Bellevue itself could use a few more blacks
and Asians; there are virtually none among the library users.
White is not necessarily bland, but in this very white dream
library, there seems to be that something missing ... something to make it complete as an American dream. Something
that is found in the third dream library, the Chinatown Branch
of the San Francisco Public.

It's a lovely library crowd scene here, as crowded as
the other two, but different in atmosphere and in some other
respects. It does not have everything; it desperately needs
money for materials, staff, and refurbishing. It is out of
space. It lacks Chinese-language children's media. Because
the boundaries of the community it serves are impossible to
determine, its per capita circulation cannot be accurately
measured. But in intensity of use, it's got to be among the
top few branch libraries in all of America. From the look
of things, its materials weren't being read--they were being
devoured. The patronage of the Chinatown Branch is about
98 percent Chinese, and--although even the most positive
racial stereotypes must be avoided--I wickedly thought of that

Chinatown--a favorite branch in Everybody's Favorite City.

"About half the adult materials are Chinese, and immigrants turn up at the (Chinatown Branch, SFPL) library their second week in the country."

"love of learning" traditionally associated with the Chinese culture. The children in the library had just come from public school, and in an hour would be off to Chinese school, their daily routine. You'd have thought this to be the one interlude for a little hell raising. Instead, their "misbehavior" was typified by the young girl who said to us, her arms full of books, "The librarian must hate me--I borrow about ten things a day!"

Branch librarian Stella Chan loves her dearly, and had to agree with our generalization; for keeping up with that thirst for learning in terms of Chinese-language and other materials occupies a great deal more of her energies than official

Librarian Stella Chan at her Chinatown Branch, SFPL. For intensity of use, it may be unsurpassed in America.

duties warrant. On the one hand, it's a dream situation, for
she identifies with her patrons, who know her well, know
each other, and enjoy a family-like atmosphere in the library;
on the other, it's an almost impossible one, since right now
she handles Chinese-language technical and reader services
as well as the administration of the branch.

It wasn't always a dream library. Up to 1968, the
collection (and librarian) was Anglo, and the Chinese community used it little. Then Chinese librarian Judy Yung took
over, and word began to spread that Chinese materials--se-
lected from Hong Kong and Taiwan catalogs and local book-
stores--were available. Now, about half the adult materials
are Chinese, and immigrants turn up at the library their second week in the country. There are still many special acquisitions problems. For instance, a recent influx of Tai-
wanese people has increased the demand for Mandarin works.

One interesting aspect of American library life in the
branch is that the children's librarian is black and has ex-
posed the Chinese children to aspects of black culture as well
as serving their other interests. California civil service
laws are such that all black librarians cannot always be
placed in "black" branches, nor all Chinese professionals in
Chinatown. There are some means by which ethnic needs
and the librarians to fill them can be matched, but to many
in the system, it's still too difficult to skirt seniority and
rank and other civil service elements in making these place-
ments. Yet, when one sees a meeting of cultures in branches
like Chinatown, it doesn't look so bad.

What does look bad are the musty furnishings creating
an institutional look of forty years ago. Some revenue sharing funds are marked for refurbishing the branch, but to see

the authentic Great American Dream Library Interior, you
have to go down the hill, cross the Golden Gate Bridge, and
drive a few minutes in Marin County to the charming town of
Mill Valley, which we did.

"You must see the Mill Valley library!" We were
told that by everyone from a school teacher who takes a
morning Tai-Chi class on the library's terrace to a writer
enamored of its enormous wood-burning fireplace. Librarian
Thelma Percy enjoys other dreamy qualities about her library:
the small Mill Valley community (about 13,000) supports it
religiously and generously, declining membership in the county system; the collection of 80,000 volumes is a good one,
used to the hilt; and the patrons are so interesting--artists,
writers, old timers. But what freaks all visitors, users or
not, is the setting of the long, low 1966 building in a small
forest of redwoods, some of them growing through holes cut
in the deck, most of them visible through glass doors and
windows, along with dogwoods, California maples, ivy, ferns,
azaleas, rhododendrons, and so on. These wonders are
viewed from the comfort of custom-designed walnut lounge
chairs, matching the soft, woody textures elsewhere and
warmed on chill nights by burning pine in that baronial fireplace. It could make one give up television.

Yes, the Good Life, even as dreamed by the most
Dionysian of us, can be enjoyed in a West Coast library.
Near the golden, mustard-covered vineyards of the upper
Napa Valley, an hour north of San Francisco, is the St. Helena Public Library and its Napa Valley Wine Library. From
a fairytale stucco building put up in 1907, librarian Betty
Reed provides a good range of general services and oversees
her special library, which was founded in 1961 and has been
directed since 1963 by the Napa Valley Wine Library Associa-

The much-loved 1907 building housing the St. Helena Public
and Napa Valley Wine Library, about an hour's drive north
of San Francisco. Librarian Betty Reed, left, founded the
special wine library in 1961.

tion (open membership: $5). The separate room housing
the wine collection is as sunny and charming as some of the
vintner's tasting rooms nearby--but here one tastes of several hundred valuable monographs on wine, French ampelo-
graphies, wine periodicals, pamphlets, engravings, maps,
bills of lading, photographs of wine festivals, vanished wineries, interviews with vintners, and, of course, labels. It's
a dreamy, marvelous little sanctuary, though it's becoming
widely known. Local users range from executive chemists
at the big wineries to the young "amateur" vintner browsing
through some magazines, who told us, "My wine is pretty
crappy--but this place is just about the greatest thing going."

Inside the Napa Valley Wine Library. Said this patron: "My wine is pretty crappy--but this place is just about the greatest thing going."

"Golden California kids...." One of them takes part in an
origami class at El Granada Library, San Mateo County (see
frontispiece).

And at the end of our dreams--for some of us, any-
way--there is a little library by the sea....

The El Granada Library of San Mateo County, a few
hundred breathtaking cliffs south of San Francisco, is across
the street from the Pacific Ocean. It's just a one-room joint
that you enter like a saloon, but it's so packed with good
things to read and see that one could stay here for years, a
Lotus reader, just glancing through the window every so often
at the sea and sky, backdrop for the dream. Sometimes the
staff members feel that way, but the tremendous library use
by the community's 5,000 people leaves little time for rev-
eries. The circulation desk looked like the A&P checkout.
Golden California kids were piling out of pickup trucks and
into the library, almost needing those trucks for the volume
of books they were taking out. It seems there's not much
else to occupy the mind at leisure in El Granada, not even
TV, for the reception is poor. A librarian's dream, some
would say, although it might end soon; cable TV has come.

But does TV necessarily dissipate the dream? The
white-collar and blue-collar workers who make the San Fer-
nando Valley their home couldn't be a more tube-tied category
of people, could they? Everyone in the L. A. area seems
TV-crazy, but the Valley residents are suburban victims, the
most vulnerable. Yet, the West Valley Branch of the LAPL
is said to be the highest circulating branch in the nation, and
its long, terminal-like interior is filled every night. Librarian Marion Duane, originally from the East, finds this high
use dreamy enough, but she's concerned about a circulation
drop of 820,000 down to 625,000 for 1972/73. Still, she feels
the library is giving good and meaningful service that ought
not be subject to constant measurement ("doctors don't measure every service"). She notes that there are far more adult

than "juvenile" users in this branch (which serves as a regional center for several small communities) and more use of nonfiction than fiction materials.   These are generally happy aspects of library life.   There are problems here, too, such as no more space and no expandability; but compared with the nightmares of some urban libraries, West Valley is such stuff as library dreams are made on.

The Nightmares

You can love a thing to death.

And that's just what's happening with the Rufus B. von KleinSmid Central Library at the heart of the Los Angeles Public Library system.

Los Angeles loves the 1926 central building so much as a historical, sentimental landmark of something or other that for a decade the idea of a new building has been rejected as out-and-out sacrilege.

The architectural critic's statement that it's the city's only salient historical building may be true in light of L. A. 's youth and its indiscriminate waves of new construction.   But it's still no architectural masterpiece.   Why, in the East we tear down classier railroad stations every day.   What makes it seem all the more precious is that it's entirely surrounded by new, monolithic skyscrapers.   In comparison, it does have soul, character, a touch of the past, an aesthetic/cultural ambiance.   It has also been found to be a firetrap.   The spaces between the floors of stacks would provide perfect ventilation for an instant inferno, and experts estimate it would take millions to make it safe.   In addition, as popular Los Angeles Times columnist Art Seidenbaum pointed out recently, it's ill lit, overcrowded, without parking, and facing

At the heart of the Rufus B. von KleinSmid Central Library, Los Angeles Public Library System. So beautiful, the city won't give it up for a much-needed new main library building.

LAPL's Central Library: "It does have soul, character...."

City Librarian of Los Angeles, Wyman Jones.

a 5-percent budget cut that, for openers, would close its
famous children's room.

With so much money floating around the miracle miles
of Los Angeles, the library is surprisingly high and dry.
Of course, all city budgets are hard pressed, but the century-
old library seems firmly established as the poor orphan of
the municipal family.   The police get some $161 million to
about $12 million for the busiest circulating system (some
13 million items a year) of the Western world.

The central building is not the only headache that
makes City Librarian Wyman Jones earn his salary, one of
the highest in the land for public librarians.   He's got 61

branches to worry about, most of which are old, inadequate
wrecks without air conditioning or even drinking fountains.
"The vandalism is so bad we need a monthly report to keep
track of it, " he told us.   Arson, earthquakes, unions, and
obstacles to successful bond issues are other demons in his
nightmares.   "Man, we couldn't even raise enough matching
funds to get the big federal dough in the 'sixties. "

Where are the answers to these and the more technical
problems faced by large libraries?   For one thing, "The research in graduate library schools is zilch, " says Jones.
"We get practically nothing that's of use to us. "

In one area, he's set up his own high-level team of
researchers, and the library won't have to lay out a penny
for it.   He's convinced the University of Southern California
architectural school to take on the design of a prototype library building, the ideal library, as a term project for an
advanced course.   With expert professors and with Jones
available for consultation, the students are working out a
series of design problems from security to sound control.
"I wanted people to know what we're talking about when we
ask for better facilities, " he explained.   "if the class comes
up with something good and the board approves it--we'll use
it. "

Even so, that won't resolve all the library's night-
mares.   To do that, the slick, silver-haired, Texas-drawling
Mr. Jones may have to resort to one of his favorite hobbies:
Legerdemain.

The public library of Everybody's Favorite City, San
Francisco, has nightmares of its own.   No one knows this
better than Kevin Starr, author of the splendid and popular
historical profile, The Americans and the California Dream,
1850-1915 (Oxford, 1973), and recent mayoral appointee as

acting city librarian of San Francisco. Starr is a proud,
young, stocky, learned, hard-swearing, aristocratic San Franciscan who has weathered fairly well in the storm of controversy over his new post, which he intends to keep. To many,
the municipal problems in San Francisco are as messy as the
raw sewage that flowed recently in the strike of city workers.
Some have felt that Starr is part of the problem--an old fash-
ioned political appointment, a non-librarian in a post supposedly crying for a top "professional." Starr is out to
prove them wrong, even if he has to earn a library degree
to add to his Harvard Ph.D., which he is now doing as fast
as he can at Berkeley. 14 But in the meantime, he must
wrestle with budgetary nightmares similar to those of so
many other urban administrators. In February, Mayor Alioto's
projected budget for SFPL, 1974-75, was $5 million, at least
$2 million beneath "the minimum needed to continue basic
services," according to the library's figures.

"San Francisco is tremendously over-extended," Starr
told us, "because it grew up thinking of itself as a big city.
It may have a million and a half by day, but only 350,000
voters. It looks so small from the air, hardly big enough
for, what, twenty-seven library branches, three museums,
an opera, and so on. Its big middle class doesn't have the
bucks that cultural institutions are striving for. The property
owners aren't that rich. And you know, real growth must
come from the private sector. Other energies are going to
go into things like public transit and housing. And maybe they
should.

"Look," he said, grinning through a bad head cold,
"I'm a conservative, Hamiltonian kind of guy. I don't think
libraries will save civilization. I think people will save themselves. If someone gave me money for either a new library

San Francisco City Librarian Kevin Starr: "In setting the
tone for a public library, it's a question of creating a system
of excellence and mass satisfaction."

branch or better health care delivery, I think I'd sacrifice
the library.

"But," he added quickly, "I don't want any cutbacks in
present library services ... I called the mayor privately.
He didn't think any essential services will have to be cut."

On the subject of his own job and how his background
relates to the library's problems, Starr remarked, in essence:

"The library world ought to recruit people laterally,
those with appropriate expertise in other professions. Hell,
you come up through the ranks in this system, you're so
rheumy by the time you get to the top, what's the use? ...
This whole library came out of the stone age only ten years
ago.

"As for myself, I'm temporary; my goal here is to
run a large municipal institution well. And to let people ar-
ticulate themselves. Do I think this library should have a
special tone? No. San Francisco itself is not monolithic.
I've just been out visiting the branches--each is so different.
Surveys say to close slow branch libraries, but I'm against
it; it's a defiant insufficiency; it affirms the autonomy of the
neighborhood community. In setting the tone for a public library, it's a question of creating a system of excellence and
mass satisfaction."

And if Kevin Starr manages that, we later mused, he
will have snatched an American dream from the jaws of the
library's nightmares.

For the reality, asserts Effie Lee Morris, the library's
outspoken coordinator of children's services, is not at all like
the dream. "Read between the lines of all the public relations
propaganda," she advised. "This is a very personalized system. Everyone asks, what's in it for me? The bigotry is
at the heart of civil service, the heart of the city. You may

see the Third World, the swingers, on the streets, but they
don't run things.   And there are still a half-million whites
among the city's 700,000.

"The schools are terrible, and when they were deseg-
regated recently, there was a tremendous protest--Nazi uni-
forms, kids withdrawn.

"I am not anti-Starr, but neither am I afraid of anyone, or to point out another SFPL library director who did
not believe in affirmative action, who could not get the word
'black' out of his mouth.   My service concept for children
was developed in New York and Cleveland--the outreach concept.   We're understaffed for it here.   Children's services
are a budgetary afterthought.   We've at least managed to re-
evaluate the collection and free two librarians to develop an
early childhood program--federally funded.   But the branches
can't support the pre-school need.   How can my children's
librarians fulfill any of the children's rights to library service
when civil-servant branch librarians want you to stand there
and check out books?"

Carl Cox, adult services librarian at the library's
Western Addition Branch, is a black person who grew up in
the San Francisco area and has loyalties to it, but he agrees
that the civil service system has certain built-in prejudices.
He feels that patrons of all colors are getting short-changed.
His branch serves blacks, Japanese, a hospital community,
and some generally "hip young people."   His black history
programs have been moderately successful, but "the Japanese
collection is really a disgrace.   The people have read it all
and we can't get more money for it."   Earlier in his career
he worked in outreach programs for the North Star Borough
of Fairbanks, Alaska, where "they had money, staff, programs, people.   Here, there's practically none of those things,

and yet miracles are expected."

Magic by Wyman Jones; miracles by Kevin Starr.
That--along with plenty of public aid--is all it will take to
work out the problems of these two city libraries of California.   Let it not be thought, however, that because there are
nightmares, crises, and perils at every turn within the two
antiquated systems that there are not also a great many marvelous and forward looking things going on.   We've already
profiled some of the dream branches, and we'll soon describe
some activities--such as LAPL's Shut-In Service--that are
nothing short of heroic.   But we ought to sound a strong positive note at this point, and there's no better and quicker way
to do it than with miniprofiles of SCAN and BARC, two far-
out reference networks funded by Uncle Sam, but very West
Coasty in their work.

Each functions mainly as a reference back-up service
for member systems in the area, receiving questions that the
libraries can't answer.   The queries come in through a teletype communications network, are assigned to staff members,
researched, and sent back out by teletype.   The reference
teams sometimes develop a certain esprit, a style, that can
make the work a lot more humanistic than it sounds considering that researchers never meet the patrons who ask the questions.   The queries are sometimes pretty wild in themselves,
which adds to the interest, and none is considered unimpor-
tant.

The two operations are still relatively small, together
handling only about 600 questions a month; yet, they call to
mind once more that vast area of speculation: on the West
Coast as an intimation of America's future.

These are but two of dozens of reference networks
around the nation, and they are technologically child's play

compared with some of the medical information systems or other sci-tech reference networks. But the National Commission on Libraries and Information Science, now proposing a national computer network that many feel devalues everyday, public informational needs, will do no better than to incorporate the very human elements of BARC and SCAN into their design for tomorrow's American libraries.

Below, is a quick comparison of the two networks.

SCAN (Southern California Answering Network)

Founded: 1969.

Funds: LSCA I, administered by the Calif. State Library.

Research staff: 7, all subject specialists.

Director: Evelyn Greenwald.

Serves: About 400 public libraries from Santa Barbara to San Diego.

Other activities: Identifying and indexing local information sources; updating printed sources; issuing newsletter SCAN-NINGS on recent questions and "Information Bulletin" on special topics.

Style: Relatively serious, subject oriented.

Recent queries: The ranking of the Palm Springs smog level in Southern California, and the composition of the smog; the name of Teddy Roosevelt's one-legged chicken.

BARC (Bay Area Reference Center)

Founded: 1967.

Funds: LSCA I, administered by the Calif. State Library.

Director: Gil McNamee.

Research staff: 6 generalists with special subject interests.

Serves: 72 public libraries in Northern California.

Other activities: continuing education workshops for member
reference librarians; produced the prize-winning magazine
Synergy, 1967-1974, first and best of the "alternative" library
magazines (the last issue, No. 42, Winter 1973, is on BARC
itself); BARC Notes newsletter.

Style: Hardworking, high on reference; mystic; freaky in San
Francisco's freakier days, now less so.

Recent query: My diesel powered Mercedes broke down and
I can't get to work--what should I do?

Classic queries: "Most Exotic":   History of the ironing board;
"Most melancholy":   What is the life expectancy of the sea
cow?

Their Own Thing

> Everybody's got a thing
> But some don't know
> How to handle it.   --Stevie Wonder

What distinguishes so many West Coast librarians from
colleagues elsewhere in the nation is that they are the kind of
people who have said, "Why not?"

"If the West Coast is the promised land," they asked
themselves one day, "then why not be part of it myself?
Why not me?" Or perhaps it was a theme of earlier generations in the bloodline. It means these librarians are of a
stock that doesn't look for every possible excuse, every threat
to comfort and security and sameness before making the
changes that will set their lives on a new course.

Not that the West Coast settlers and unsettlers are
necessarily any better than the rest of us; for the why-not
questions have often been: Why not go out there and rape
and plunder the land? Why not find a nice white Southern
California community? Why not walk out on my responsibilities here?

But, to make a wild generalization for the Wild West:
The why-not people have been doing for 150 years what is
presently called one's "own thing," so that by now--they really know how to handle it.

Sue Rugge and Georgia Finnigan Mulligan are a pair of
dynamite Bay Area librarians who started a firm called Information Unlimited when they were laid off jobs as special
librarians. They decided to do their own thing because, although they enjoyed library research, they wanted to get away
from the job-seeking ratrace, the bureaucratic setting, and
to be more in control of their working lives.

The dynamic duo does freelance research out of one
small room in a residence, but has built up a business with
industrial and other clientele that is headed toward a gross
of $50,000 a year. Research expenses are high. There are
about eight part-time people. The proprietors pay themselves
modest salaries, but it looks as though the business is going
to make it. [15]

The two women, who happen to be very charming and
appealing in person, have succeeded in business by really trying, by combining pure West Coast aggressiveness and why-
notness with solid subject and research expertise. But also:
"As women working in the business world, which is predominantly male, we felt we had to psych out the people we were
talking to. If they were fatherly, we were sweet girls who
needed their help. If they were businesslike, we were just
as businesslike."

In a Bay Area Reference Center (BARC) "Workshop
on Work," Ms. Mulligan added this comment: "The two of
us really live our work, and it's not work; it's fun. It's fulfilling. It's the first time I haven't gotten depressed on Sunday nights."

San Francisco Public Library.

Others associated with BARC--which itself began as a why-not operation--talked with us about doing their own numbers as a means of self-expression, social commitment, or simply as an alternative to the 9-5 routine.

BARC staffer Johanna Goldschmid, for instance, does her own bookbinding after hours, printing the cloth, marbling the endpapers, creating complete works of art for friends and for the joy of it, as well as running classes in bookbinding for young people. It's a labor of love that projects in the way she talks about it and in the look of her work.

Linda Ramey works halftime for BARC and runs her
own shop the rest of the workday. She set it up on a whim,
but "it has really turned out to be an alternative for me. "
Her San Francisco "body shop" selling lotions, oils, and soaps
is called Common Scents and functions also as a free switchboard center for community information. Ms. Ramey's library background and interests could not have allowed it to
be otherwise.

Almost as famous as the saga of Laura **X** and her Women's History Research Center in Berkeley (sensitively described in Jane Howard's A Different Woman) is the story of
Celeste West: of how Ms. West turned BARC's thing, Synergy, into her own thing to the delight of many, and how she
ultimately left BARC to form her own thing's own thing, Book-
legger Magazine, an independent journal for librarians.
Whether or not Booklegger--which had about 1, 000 subscrip-
tions as we talked to its editor--will survive is hard to say;
but Ms. West, a staunch feminist, a tough customer with a
militantly independent life style, is likely to be saying why
not (and other choice epithets) for some time to come.

"I don't think I could be doing what I'm doing without
a library background, " we were told by Barbara Pruett, librarian for the United Farm Workers at union headquarters
in Keene, Calif. But it was pretty certain she could be making what she's making without it: she earns about $5 a week
and a room for providing a full-time information service to
union officials who, in turn, aid and inform the workers in
their struggle for a better life. Ms. Pruett (who now gets
a few additional pennies for expenses from the SRRT/People's
Librarian Task Force's Adopt-A-Librarian program) puts in

San Francisco Public Library.

about nine hours a day and many nights and Sundays. She believes in the workers' causes, has made their thing her own; but she feels that direct library service to the people in the fields is practically a waste of time. Many don't read, and those who can are too tired at the end of a day. The information files she maintains for union staff, however, have often proved useful in supporting the worker cause and are valued by the union leadership. Cesar Chavez uses them personally from time to time.

Martin Zonligt, who came to California from Utah, has also done his own thing for library service to migrant workers. His proposal to study the information needs of such workers on the West Coast earned him a small grant from the Council on Library Resources, Inc., and from May through July 1973 he traveled through Idaho, Washington, Oregon, California, and Texas interviewing farmworkers, former farmworkers, and librarians. He, too, found that library services direct to the people pose many problems, but unlike Ms. Pruett he does not consider them insurmountable. He recommends that libraries take the form of "survival information centers" under the direction of the workers, but with cooperation from libraries and other social agencies. Head of extension for the Stanislaus County Free Library, Modesto, Mr. Zonligt is in the heart of migrant labor country. He also heads the ALA/SRRT Task Force on Farmworkers, and ALA will soon issue his complete project report.

We read a summary of the report. It's a document of why-not thinking.

In Los Angeles, there is a small group of librarians who do their own thing by day while helping others to do theirs in the middle of the night. They are called the Nite

Owls, four reference librarians who operate the Los Angeles
PL's HOOT-OWL Ready Reference Service, answering about
70 questions between 9 p.m. and 1 a.m. during each of seven
nights a week. (The Bay Area has a similar service called
BOSS, answering about 25 a night.) The librarians at HOOT-
OWL work a part-time week--they like days for themselves--
Supervisor Barbara Edge simply to "live her own life style"
after many years as a full-time reference librarian; Eileen
Brady in order to write TV scripts (she's trying hard to
break into that market); and another to drive a truck during
the day. Although most questions that come in at these odd
hours are not at all odd, the librarians will proudly research
anything that a caller wants to know, whatever his nocturnal
abode or somber preoccupation.

And why not?

For Whom the Dream is Over ...

Then, too, there are those who have said, "Why not
grow old on the West Coast?" A great many, in fact, drawn
by the climate to join those born in it and who have lived
well and long. As has often been observed, old age is omni-
present here; it is an industry. From a West Coast librarian's point of view, the possibilities for meaningful service
are almost unlimited, but the funds for it are as stingy as in
the most threadbare Eastern poverty pockets. And that means
calling out the volunteer brigades.

One of the most successful volunteer shut-in-service
programs in the nation is that of the Los Angeles Public Library. Led by such dedicated librarians as its present director, Betty Gay, the service has grown to hundreds of volunteers bringing many thousands of items to shut-ins--mostly

Two volunteers from the Los Angeles PL Shut-In Service (foreground) bring reading materials to this resident of a convalescent home in San Pedro--and share many of her anxieties about the passing days.

elderly--throughout the vast reaches of the L. A. system, all on a shoestring budget frayed at both ends. For big statistics don't guarantee funding, nor do they demonstrate the meaning of the right book put in the hands of one old trouper with little else to occupy the dwindling hours. The very arrival of the volunteers brightens clouded eyes, whether or not the books they bring are of any real interest. But an animated moment sans circulation figures, we all know, is no justification for library service funds.

There are few experiences more moving in this business than to follow some devoted volunteers through their rounds among elderly shut-in patrons. There's no need to dwell on what it is to be old in America, life's biggest drag however you slice it. But one quickly realizes in making these rounds the courage it takes for volunteers to overcome their own apprehensions about age, or sickness, or helplessness. Many volunteers are retired people just this side of being shut-ins themselves. In serving well, one identifies with the patrons; and in identifying, one shares anxieties all too close to home. And so it was cheery courage, not fear, that we observed in volunteers Betty DeMasi and Phyllis Ackerman, both former librarians, as they visited residents of a convalescent home in San Pedro, Calif. The two women are, in a word, fantastic; the kind of volunteers who make library extension services a dream, who bring to life the American dream of people helping one another for the sheer satisfaction of it, and, in the process, who provide book-inspired dreams for those whose lives can no longer engender them.

San Pedro is a port town in the L. A. area, and in the convalescent homes are many old seamen and others who have lived by the sea. The "guest" home we visited is called Harbor Crest, a shipshape operation with portholes in its dining room. But not every resident wants books about the sea.

"The key thing," said volunteer Ackerman, "is to keep your mouth shut and listen to their interests."

"But shut-ins," we learned from the volunteers, "are at first shy, suspicious, wondering what the price is. Many say, 'Oh, I'm too nervous to read.' It's taken as long as three-and-a-half months to get one to accept a book. Others can't get enough. One woman from the Soviet Union reads five languages. Another shut-in has had a library card since 1911."

Because of good training and organization in the LAPL

Service to Shut-Ins, volunteers are able to choose materials
based on their own interpretations of patron needs.

"She gives you anything you want, I can tell you that,"
said one Harbor Crest resident of his volunteer. "She knows
the people's character."

And from a member of a group so often denied individual character and personality, that isn't a bad tribute.

There are other good volunteer shut-in services on the
West Coast, among them one in San Mateo, Calif., headed
by Karl Reeh and called L. O. V. E. (Library Outreach Volunteers, Etc.). Mr. Reeh, like Ms. Gay, is young, dedicated,
and enthusiastic. His federally-funded project of the Peninsula Library System helps give the bedridden, the handicapped,
the blind, and the elderly a chance to reach beyond their otherwise limited horizons and to share at least vicariously in
the Western American Dream.

Or Never Was ...

When shut-in means <u>locked</u> in, that dream may well
be one that never was and never will be. For on the West
Coast as in most of the country, prison equals punishment
for a life of failed dreams, not rehabilitation or even the information with which to dream anew.

There are happy exceptions. For instance, under
Richard Hongisto, liberal, enlightened sheriff of San Francisco County, a library service for prisoners has been free to
grow from a library class project at Berkeley to a partially-
funded program of the San Francisco Public Library. Gilda
Perolman is a young SF PL staffer who coordinates the program in addition to her other duties. A native Easterner
with Eastern intensity and the why-not attitude of her adopted

"There are those West Coast children for whom the future and the dream are still open ended, for whom the library is still a place of discovery. This student in the posh Katella High School Library (Anaheim) discovers the genie of the computer....

West Coast, she points with pride to the small but significant service to some 500 short-term prisoners. The value of such service can rarely be measured except in terms of the prisoners' enthusiasm, which is high; but every so often there's a high for librarians, too: When SFPL's Ann Kincaid found some money for law books in the women's facilities, one woman who used them claimed she had three charges dropped as a result.

Another happy exception to the usual "prison" reading room is the library of the Youth Service Center of King County, Wash., a cooperative venture between the county library

... Just as this young man does on a special terminal at the
funky Venice Branch, Los Angeles Public Library.

and other agencies. Some people would be shocked to find
kids who are charged with pimping, prostitution, theft, incest,
running from home, etc., lounging about on overstuffed pil-
lows, playing the latest rock on a big juke box, and reading
Pimp or hot rod mags or whatever they ask for in this, the
library of a correctional institution. But the enlightened law
enforcement officials of this area are behind it all the way.
Librarian Sue Madden's hip, crazy, spontaneous, tough, and
loving style brings everything to life in the place, from the
very walls to the guests who stop by expecting a siege of the
institutional blahs. The kids adore her; they go absolutely
bananas when she returns from an absence. As a result, she
has turned a great many of them on to library materials,

taking them from "where they are" in the best tradition of
individualized education.   Sophisticated at the street level,
several of the youths have not had even a basic exposure to
children's books, so that some teenagers are freaked by pup-
pet shows and readings of The Three Billy Goats Gruff.

"I used to try to turn them on to libraries in general, "
said the fast-talking Ms. Madden, a Portland native who
sounds like a New Yorker, "but they'd try one on the outside,
come back, and tell me: 'You lied. ' Now I only try to turn
'em on to books. "

... Or Hasn't Yet Begun

At the other extreme are those West Coast children
for whom the future and the dream are still open-ended and
for whom the library is still a place of discovery, not re-
covery from false starts.   In our relatively short visits to
school libraries of the Coast, we saw some heartwarming instances of ordinary children--of all races--being given the
very best there is.

For instance, all the Seattle Public Schools have libraries with professional librarians.   And, behind the leadership of Marilyn Christie, supervisor of library services,
they have imaginative, flexible programs and have been able
to hold on to talented librarians like Mary Henry.

Ms. Henry is librarian at the South Shore Middle
School, which has torn down not only racial walls in its mul-
tiracial neighborhood, but the walls which literally separate
the library from the classrooms.   South Shore is an experiment in open-classroom architecture, and, except for a few
low shelves that act as boundaries here and there, it's all
one lively family of 1, 200 in one enormous, modern, carpeted

room. The library is in a well in the center of traffic, and you can't go for a drink of water without falling into it and happening on to some of its colorful, up-to-the-minute, please-touch educational resources. The all-day, instant accessibility of the library makes for heavy use of the materials; some children who could barely open Webster's Unabridged were operating AV equipment like old hands, unsupervised, unperturbed as we poked cameras at them and watched them read, view, take notes, learn. Not that the experiment in openness wouldn't often drive Ms. Henry and the teachers straight up the walls if there were any, for the line between chaos and freedom is no less thin on the West Coast than elsewhere; but the students seem to be headed in the right direction to find their share of the dream.

South Shore Middle School, Seattle, is an experiment in open-classroom architecture. The library is in a well at the center of traffic, and you can't go for a drink of water without falling into it.

Survival In The Desert

The libraries of the Seattle Public Schools are the happy beneficiaries of a sizable local tax levy, and, like those libraries benefiting from federal funds, they are able to create what we have called library life as opposed to mere survival. Money makes the difference. Tear out this paragraph and bring it to your legislators. Money makes the difference! There are no two ways about it.

But there are more ways than one to raise a few bucks, and some of the most agonizing and yet inspiring stories are of libraries that were determined to keep digging when school, local, State, and federal wells seemed bone dry.

There is a little library almost lost in the desert just outside the corridors that bring West Coast fortunes into Las Vegas every Friday evening. It is the library of the St. Viator School, a Catholic elementary and junior high school with Spanish architecture, a vandalism problem, an Episcopalian librarian with a Jewish husband, and sixteen volunteer mothers--in short, a perfect piece of Americana that we had visited a little earlier than we did our other Western American stopoffs.

Five years ago there was simply no library budget at St. Viator. The library was a closet with a shelf of books. Up to two years ago, the budget was $500 for library resources and services to about 300 students. Today, out of this arid dust has sprung a Resource Center worthy of the name, with some 3,000 up-to-date books, a bright and modern room, AV equipment, some Title II money, and a corps of painstakingly trained aides to give the students individual attention.

The difference was Librarian Blanche Zucker, who has

given full-time-and-more of her skills; an enthusiastic principal; and those sixteen volunteer mothers who, as Ms. Zucker
put it, "take their job as seriously as any for which they
might be paid; in fact, they do more because they are not.
It is a thing of which we are most proud."

It isn't that the mothers have nothing else to do; this
is Las Vegas, remember?   But they believe in extending, as
much as possible, the Western vision of the American dream
to their children.   To raise money for the first AV equipment,
they worked long hours in town taking inventory, then simply
handed over their earnings to the library.   Recently, to buy
one opaque projector, the mothers organized and tended a
four-day book fair at the center whose success made for big
news in the Las Vegas papers.   It's not the sort of thing

A few of the sixteen mothers (with their children) who cared
enough about library services at St. Viator School, Las Vegas, to create this modern Resource Center for volunteer librarian Blanche Zucker and the students.

that one could look up in library literature; and yet, it's at
the very heart of library life in America: the people for
whom library survival--in the desert or wherever--is simply
not good enough.

What We Didn't See

It was time to return ... but there was so much we
hadn't seen of West Coast library life, it felt more like the
beginning than the close of our exploration. We'd met several librarians from Oregon, but we were unable to visit that
beautiful and progressive State; we had never set foot in a
college or university library; we had not ferreted out more
examples of abysmal, backward library service as a balance
to those instances of the great American Library Dream fulfilled....

And so on. For one reporter to paint a portrait of
American Library Life in all its complexity and diversity on
those few days a year he can escape from the office--hell,
it's like tackling the Sistine Chapel on a coffee break. Even
if he were given the time, energy, and talent, there is no
guarantee that the end result would be michelangelesque in
unity, or in grandeur and holiness. For the view that library
life in America is an unholy mess is held by quite a few who
believe they understand the total picture. Just listen to them
at conferences, read them in the literature.

From what I have now seen for this series--and it
isn't all, but it's first-hand--I partly disagree. That libraries are a mess, or in a mess, may be true. To be human
is to be messy, to live by trial and error, to make mistakes,
to be well-intentioned screw-ups. We are messy about the
way we fund our libraries, the way we measure their services,

the way we define their goals. But that the mess is unholy
--I'm not sure. One may not find library service in every
square mile of the nation, but by and large it is as common
as police control, military presence, polluting industry, crim-
inal forces, political corruption, ineffective schooling, bigotry,
racism, censorship, poverty, greed, inflation, fear, ignorance, and all the other of our armies of the night. I find
it a religious comfort to know that even the rottenest library
somehow survives not very far away in America.

NOTES

1. As of January 1975, Cheryl had been unable to take advantage of the trainee grant due to rising costs associated with graduate education. She was still at Martinsburg, working at a lower salary than if she had earned the degree. A new state funding formula, however, will put more pressure on libraries to hire graduate librarians.

2. Frederic J. Glazer, West Virginia's energetic new library commissioner, has used controversial hard-sell techniques to promote his belief in the worth of libraries; the result, however, has been this dramatic increase in funding across the board, as he reported it to this author in January 1975:

1971 (Time of "Library Life" Visit)	1974
Local: $1,892,406	$3,558,343
State: 145,676	1,613,240
Federal: 339,118	622,236
TOTAL $2,377,200	$5,793,819

3. Early 1975 saw the network plan still moving forward, now under State Library Commissioner Jane Geske, a native Nebraskan. The commission's budget has enjoyed a healthy increase, and funds specifically for the networks are expected in two to three years. New state aid for local libraries is available, but libraries must meet special state standards to be eligible.

4. The people did not quite say "yes" to the full idea. The eight states declined to federate to the extent that individual state conferences would be abandoned, but they have agreed to meet in a Midwest regional conference every four years.

5. Pierre de Vise, "Chicago's Widening Color Gap; 1971," Integrated Education: A Report on Race and Schools, 9:6 (Nov.-Dec. 1971), 37-42.

6. Alphonse F. Trezza, "The Illinois State Library: History,

Organization, and Philosophy," Illinois Libraries, 54:4-5
(April/May 1971), 273-279.

7.   Mr. Trezza, on leave from his post in Illinois to serve
as executive secretary of the National Commission on Libraries and Information Science, provided this January 1975 updating of Illinois library system statistics: Membership includes 539 out of 551 tax-supported public libraries, plus
some 100 academic and 90 special libraries.   School libraries
are now eligible to join and about 40 have already signed up.
The John Crerar and University of Chicago Libraries are also
members of the system.

8.   For July 1974 to June 1975, the Neighborhood Information
Centers Project has been funded at $235,000 covering the
five centers (now Houston, Cleveland, Detroit, Atlanta, and
Queens Borough). After this third year of life, the centers
will have to be funded locally if they are to continue.   The
headquarters shifted from Cleveland to Houston, where the
principal investigator is David Hennington, Houston Public
Library Director.   The success of the demonstration centers
has varied from city to city, but all in all they have convinced
project people that there is a need for and a response to this
kind of service.

9.   Feeling that he no more fit the mold of a South Carolina
academic librarian than he fit those of Mississippi, John Carter is today (1975) with the Wyoming State Library.

10.   As of this updating, Mississippi is still without an accredited graduate library school.

11.   A tabular report on the Southeastern States Cooperative
Library Survey is available from Mary Edna Anders, Basic
Data Branch, Industrial Development Division, Georgia Technical Institute.   A full report was scheduled to appear during
1975.

12.   Col. Walsh is still bucking for that star, but at least
he's got thirty good years in the service as of 1975.

13.   The Selma community got both its library and auditorium.
A small auditorium was built in City Hall, and, thanks to revenue sharing funds, a new library is scheduled for completion
in 1976.   The building will contain 15,000 square feet compared with the present library's 3,700.   Donated funds also
enabled the library to begin bookmobile service Nov. 1, 1974,

and to reach the entire community area for the first time in
the library's history.

14.   Dr. Starr earned his library degree in 1974.   In addition, as he wrote to this author, "I have cured myself of the
habit of swearing and ... I am working out daily at the
Y. M. C. A. so that I might be less 'stocky.'"   He also received some windfall funds for the library with the help of
Mayor Alioto, and has begun a special program for improve-
ment of services.

15.   From a letter to the author written Aug. 21, 1974, by
Ms. Rugge and Ms. Mulligan: "Business is doing very well.
We have had some large literature searches lately and two
contracts to do some library consulting and reorganizing.
We got an office near the campus ... and hired a full-time
office manager to free our time for working on projects and
marketing."